EGYPT

PHOTOGRAPHS BY ELIZABETH KRAMER

THIS IS PART OF THE VISITING SERIES.

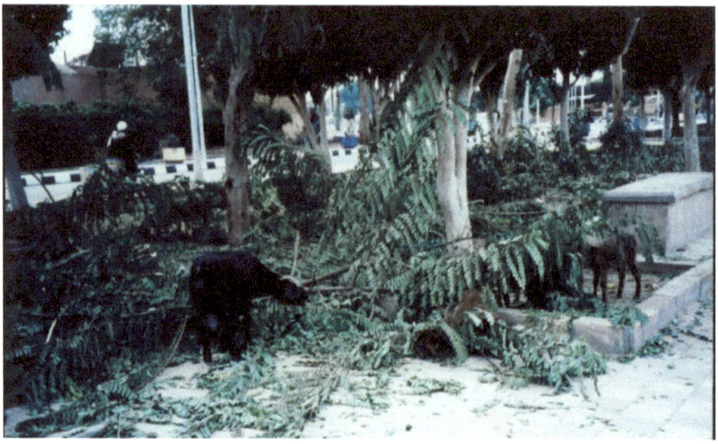

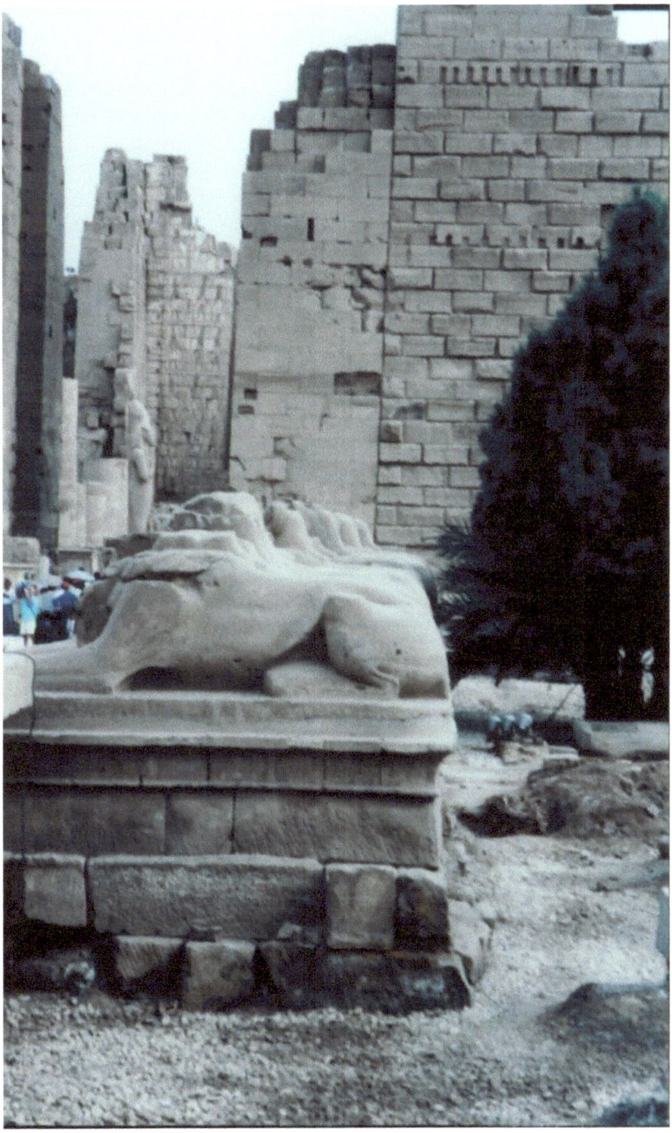

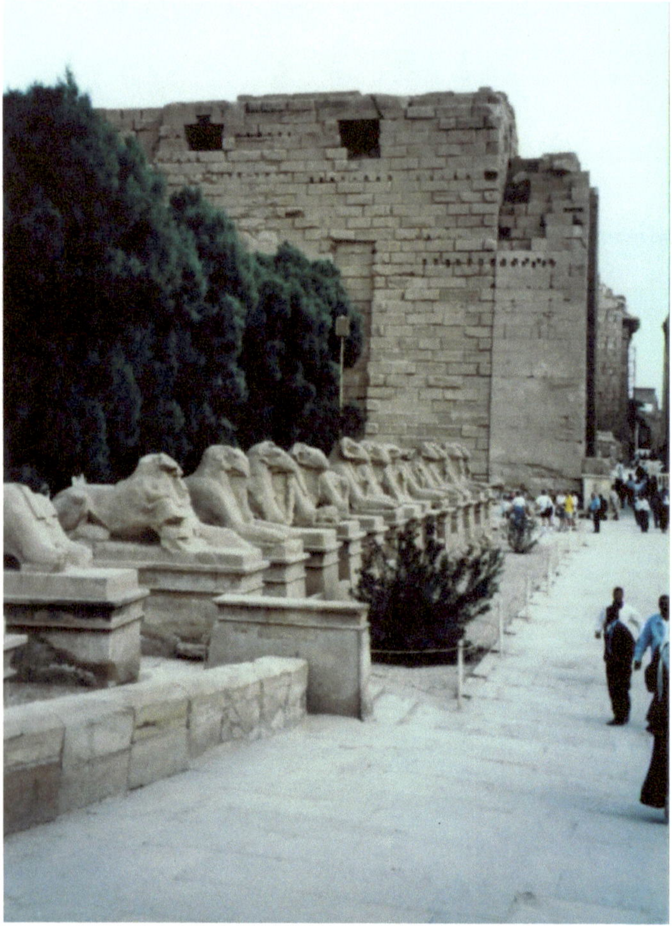

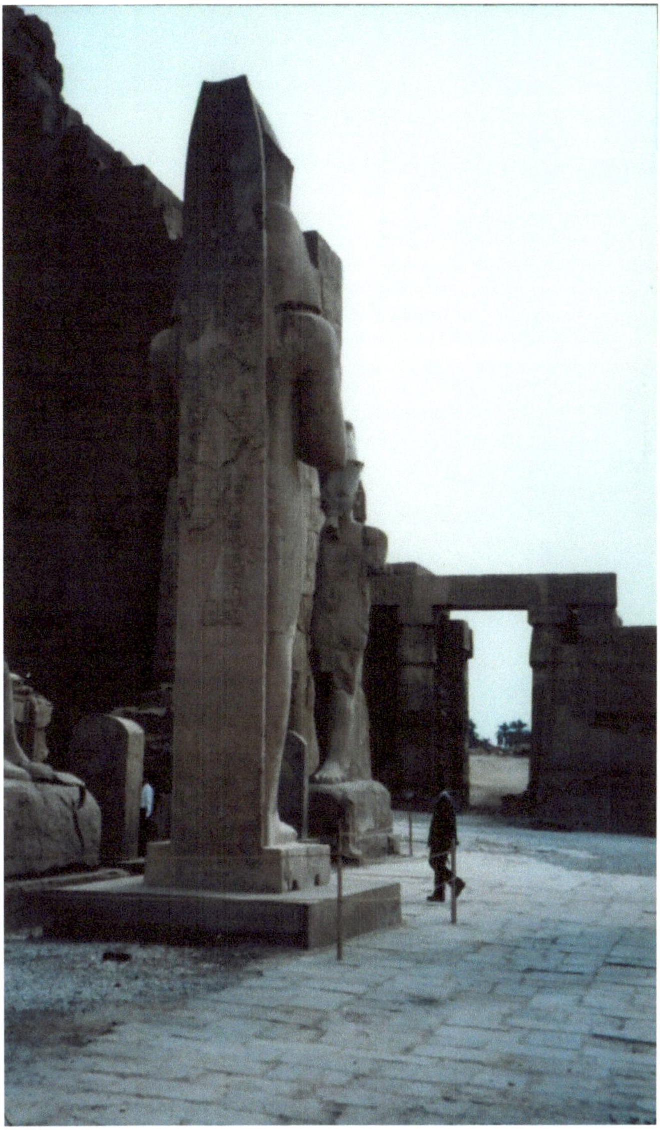

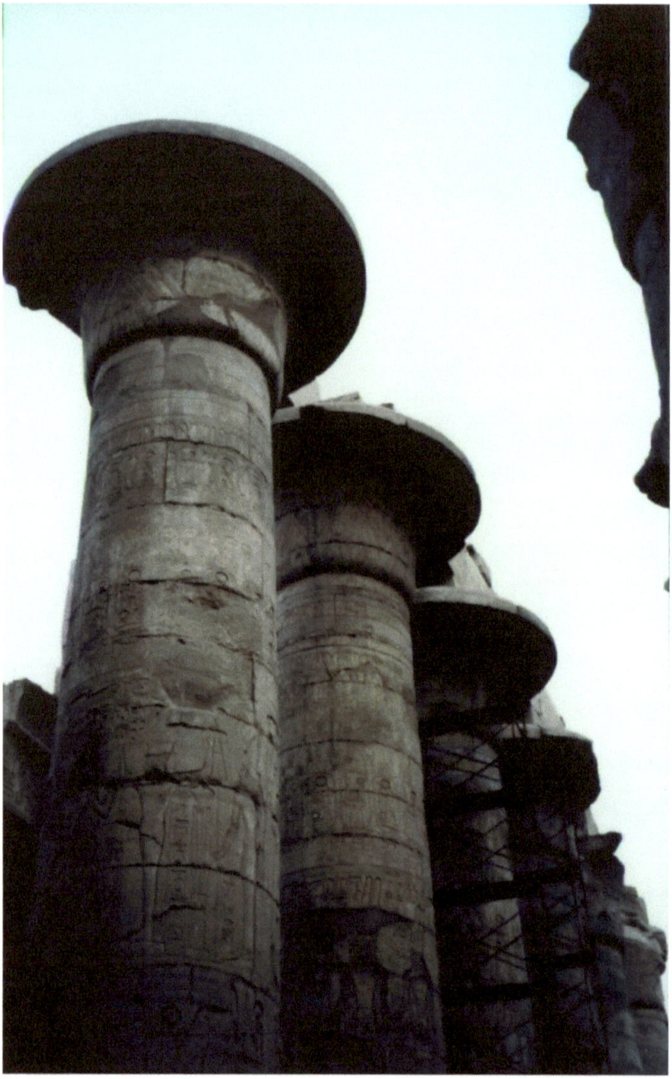

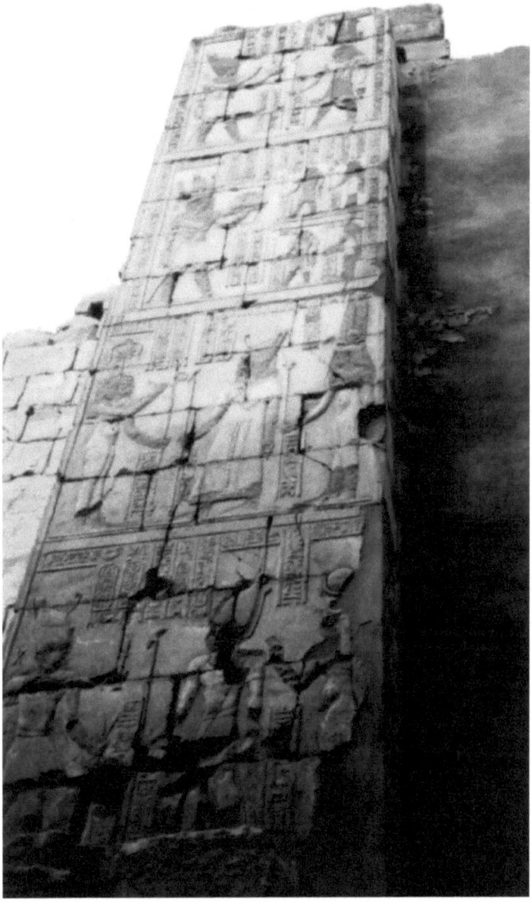

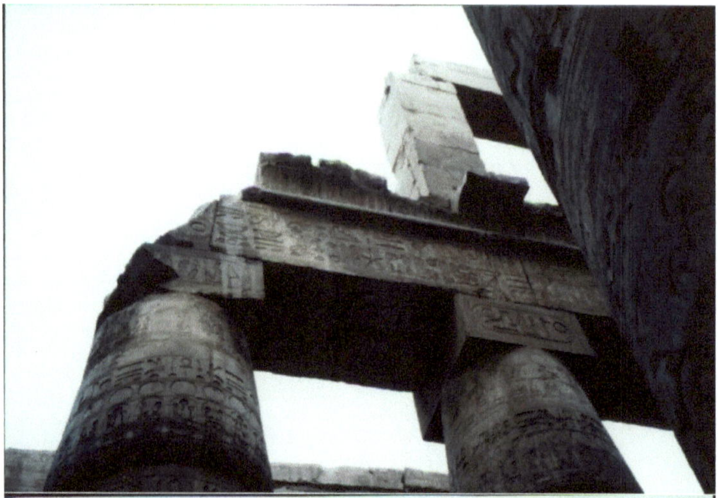

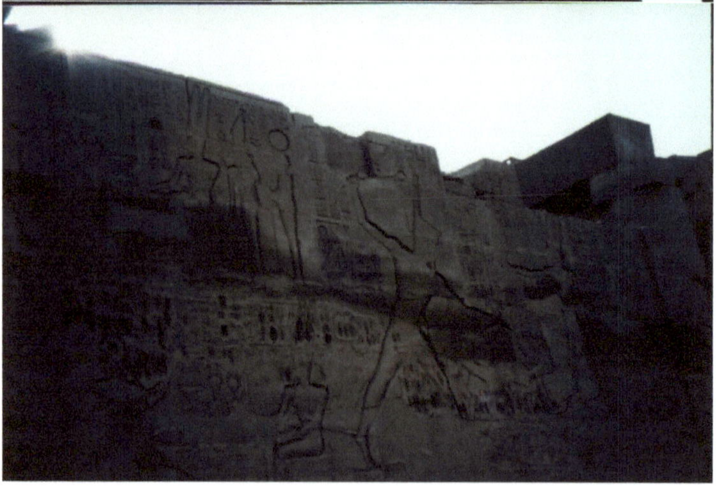

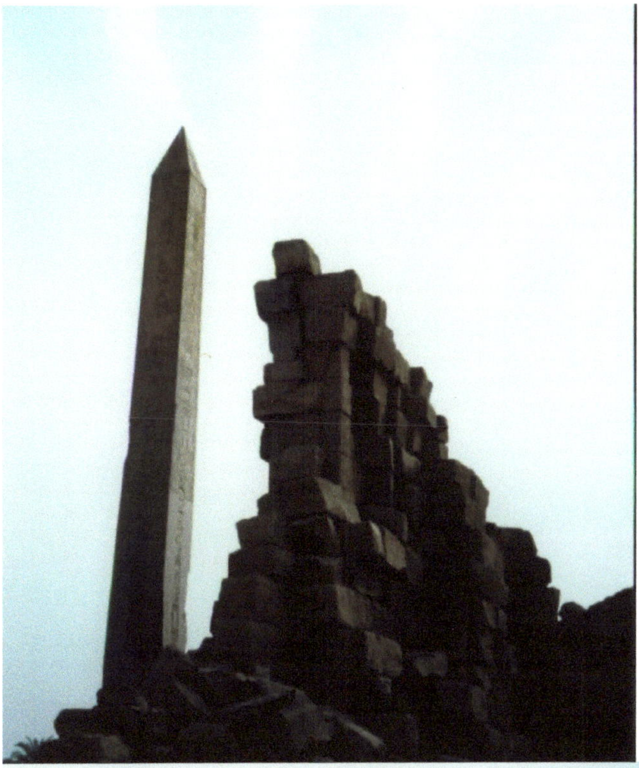

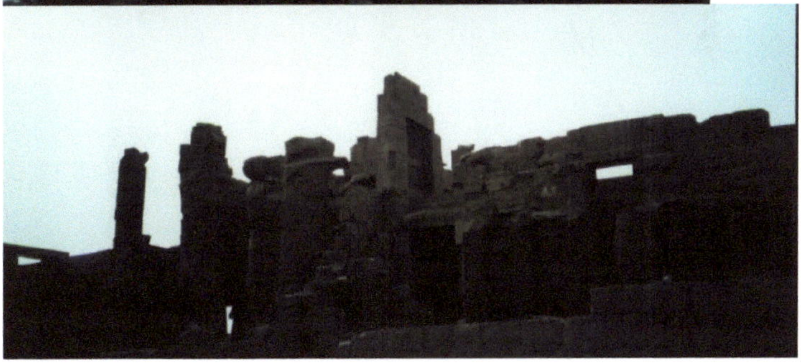

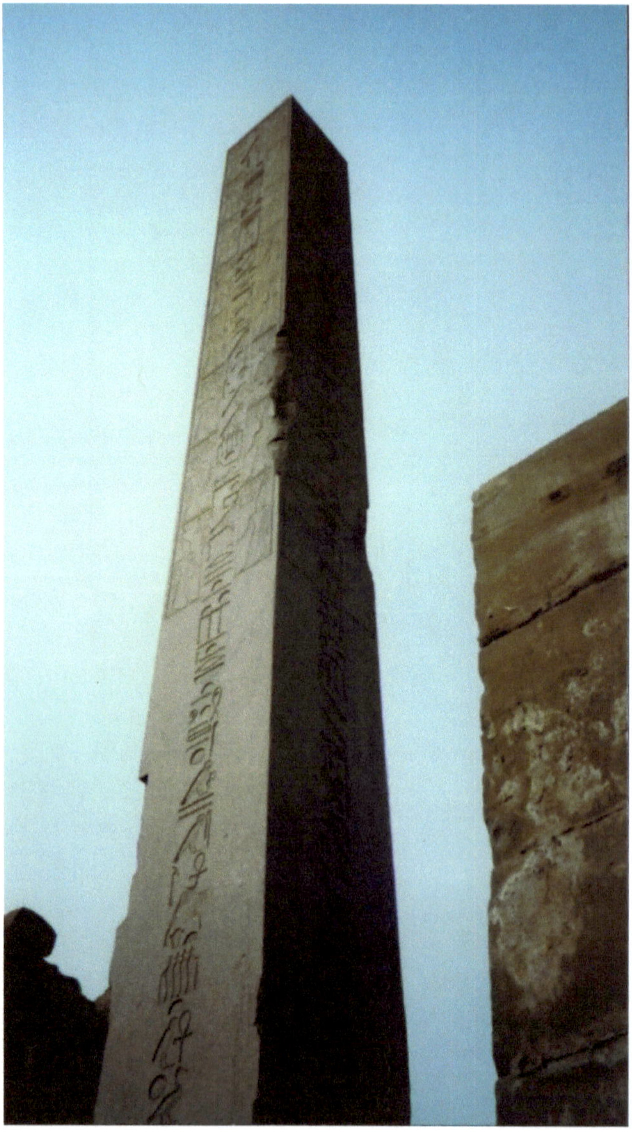

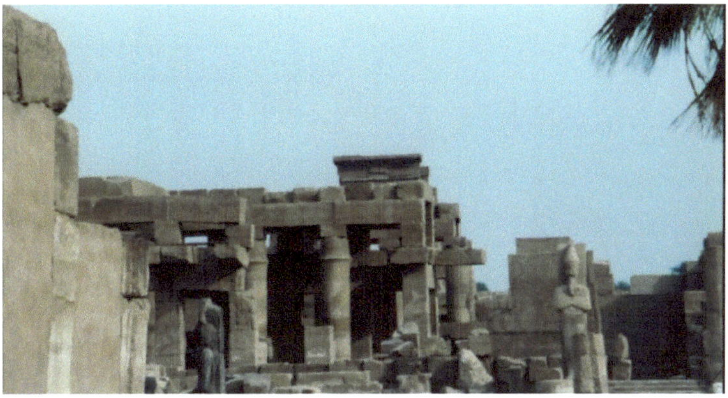

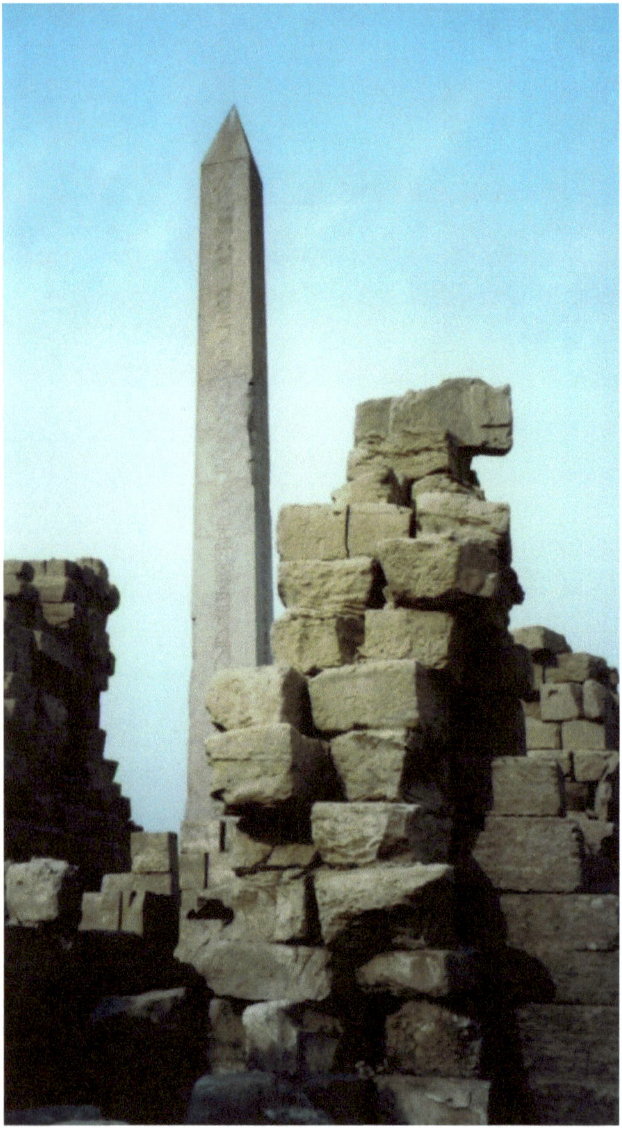

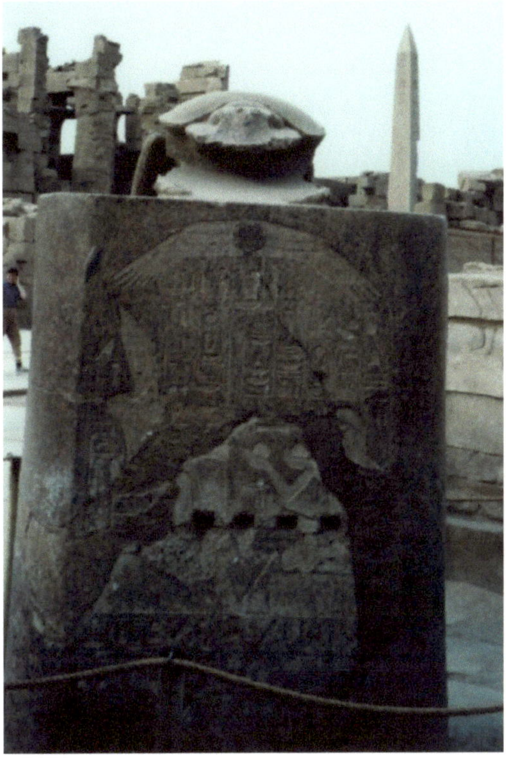

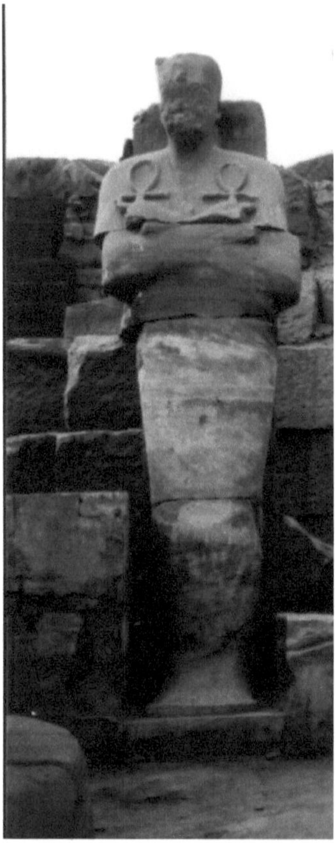

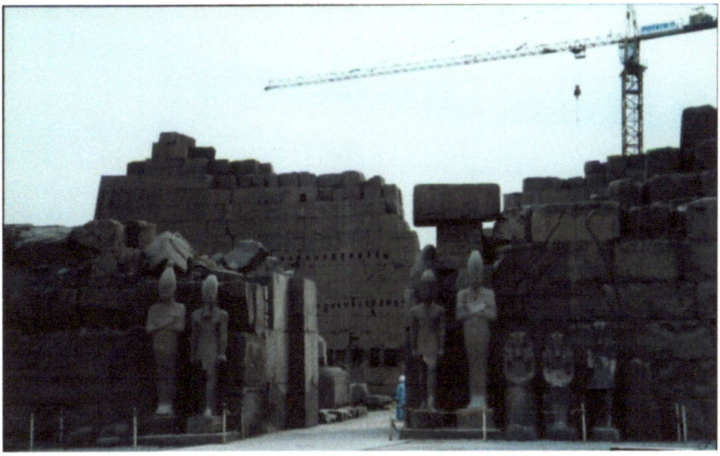

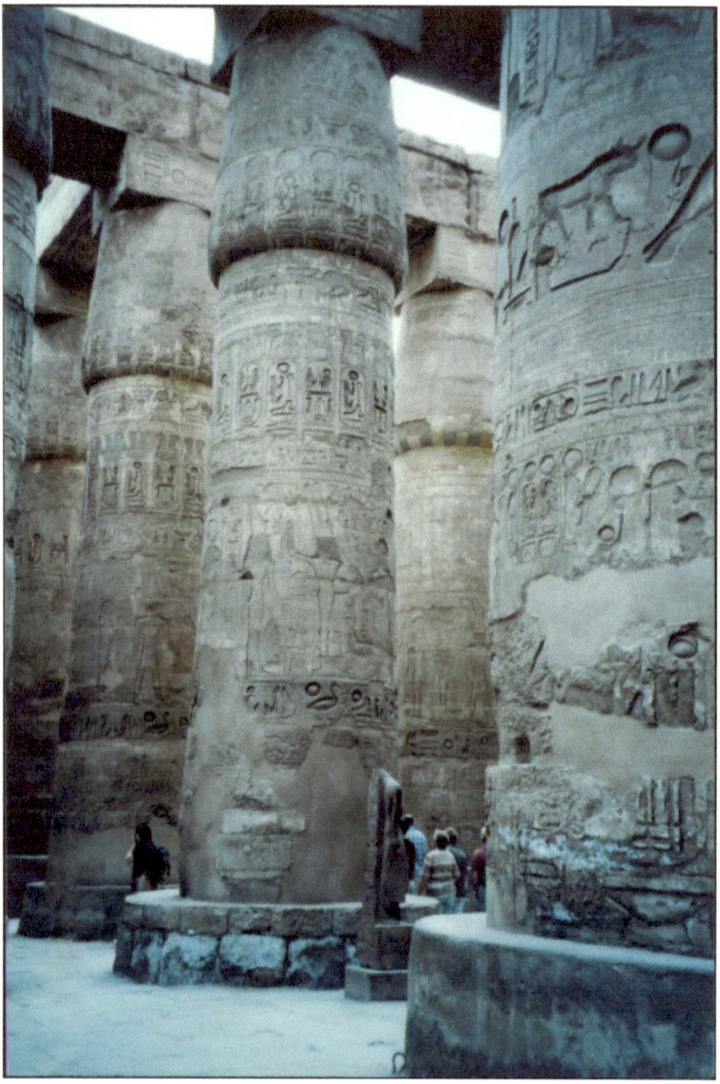

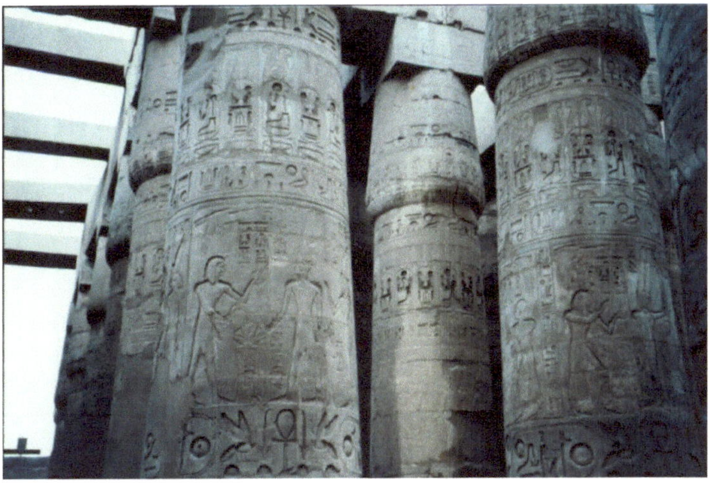

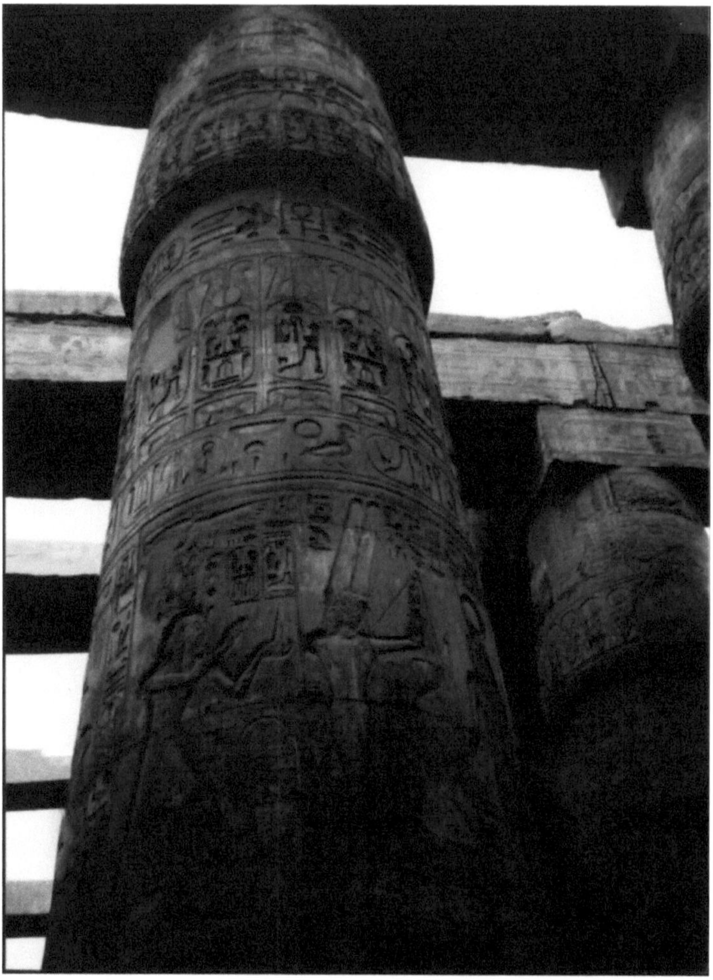

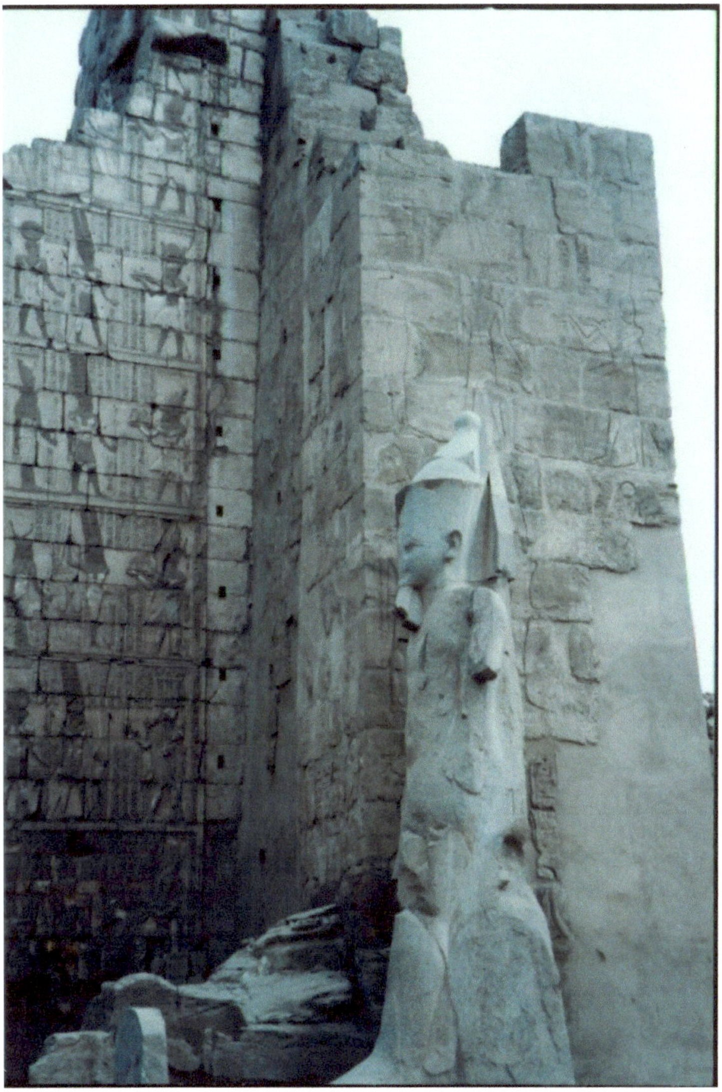

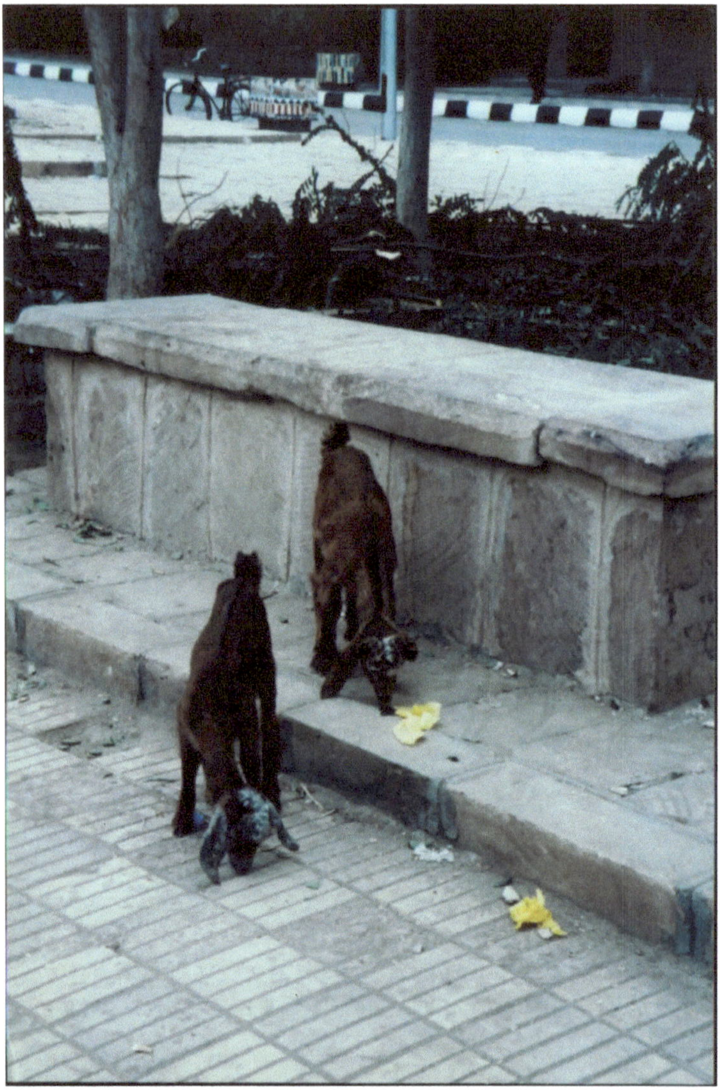

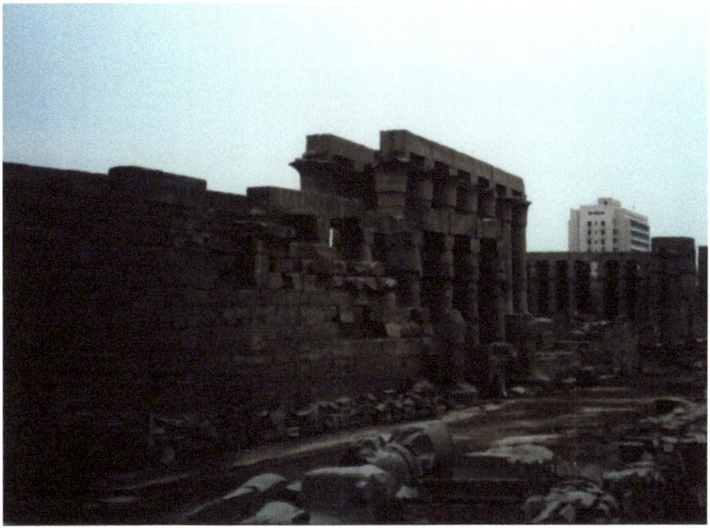

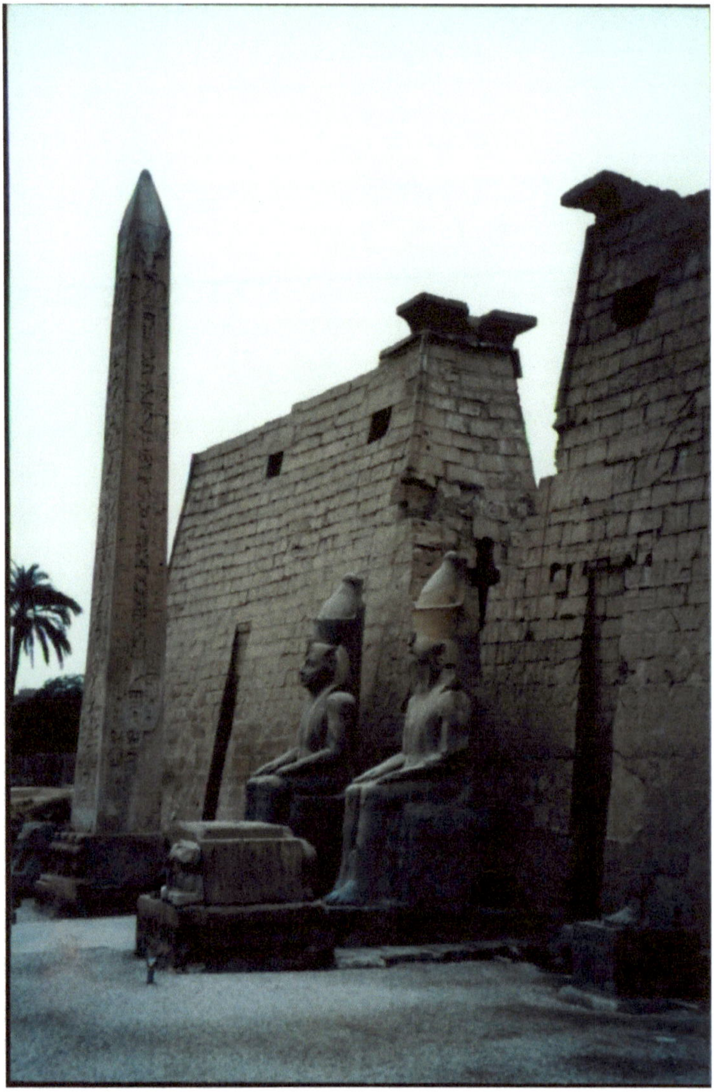

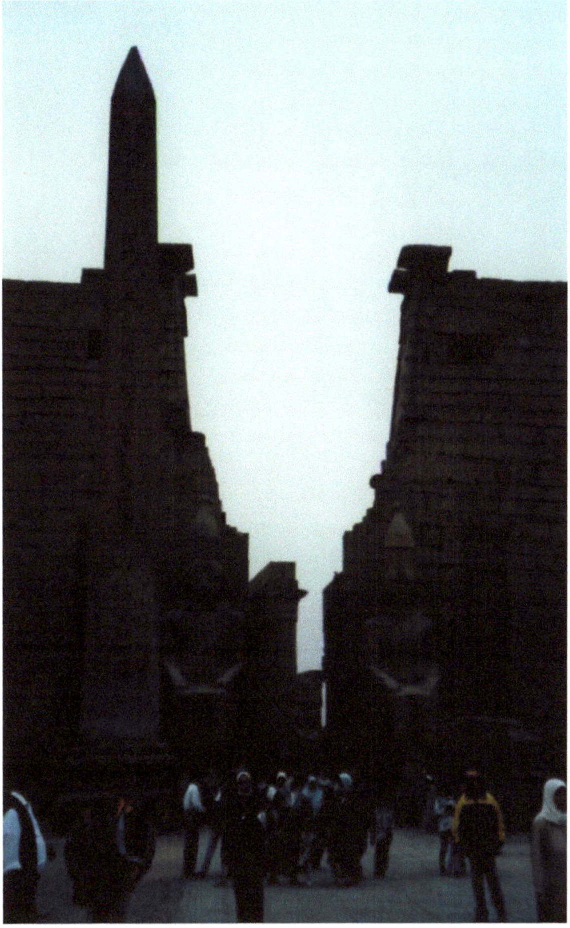

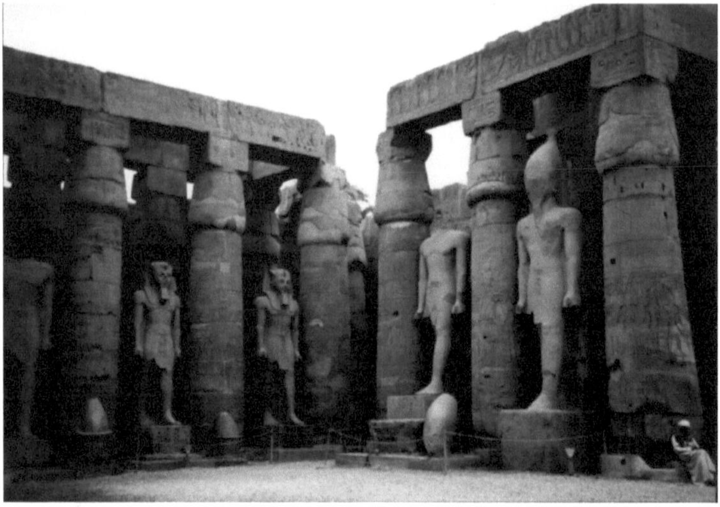

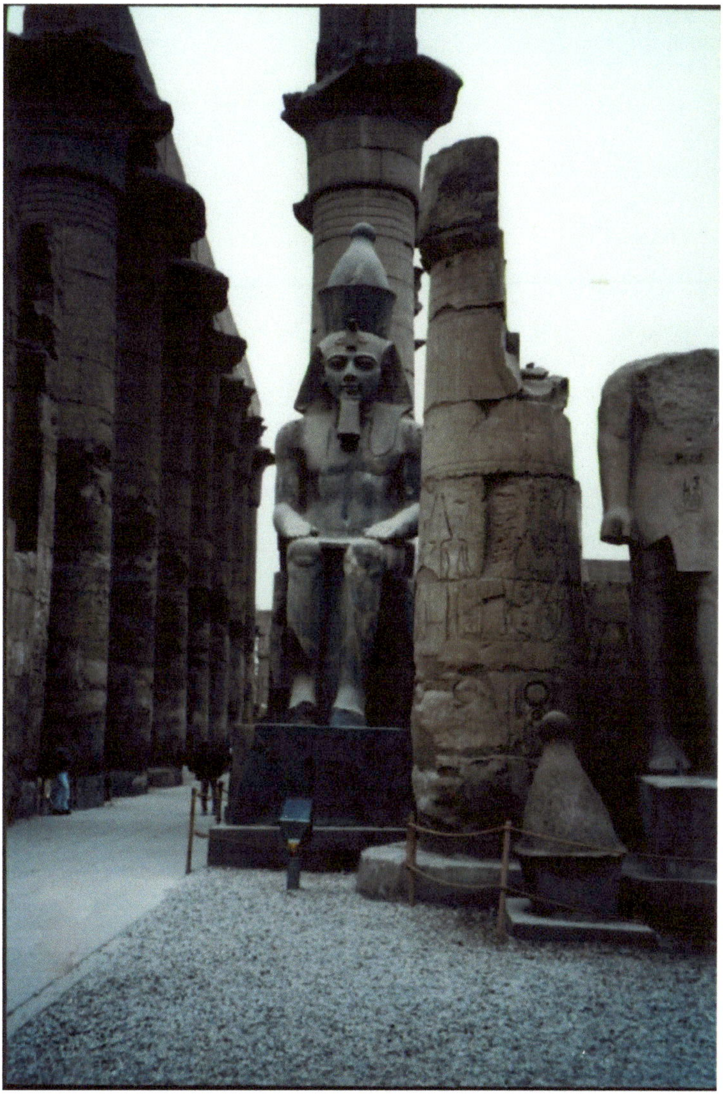

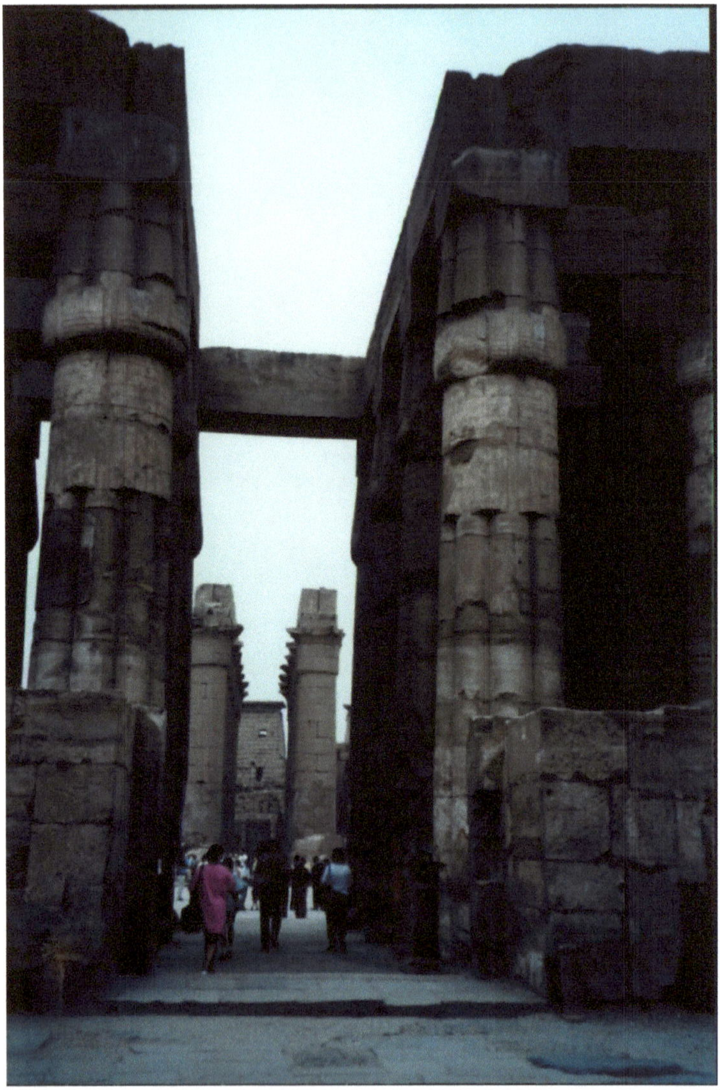

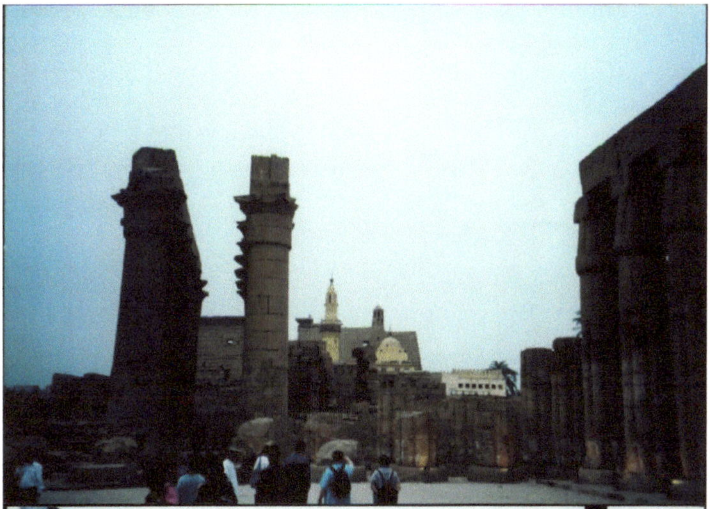

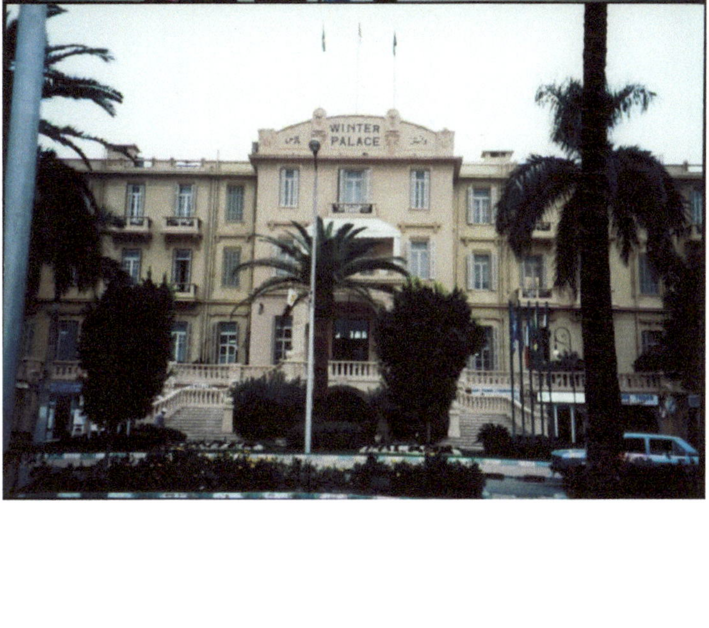
WINTER
PALACE

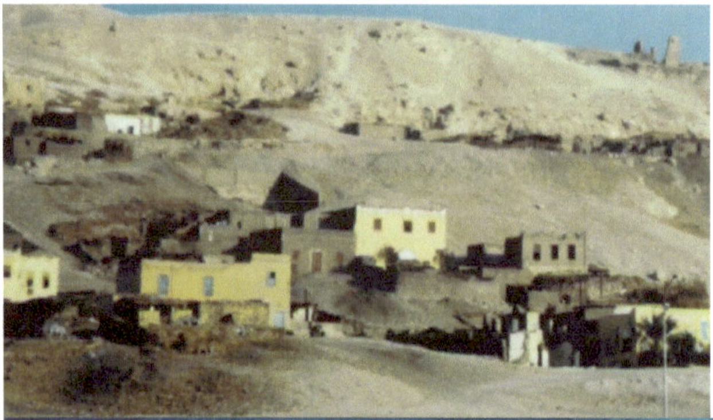

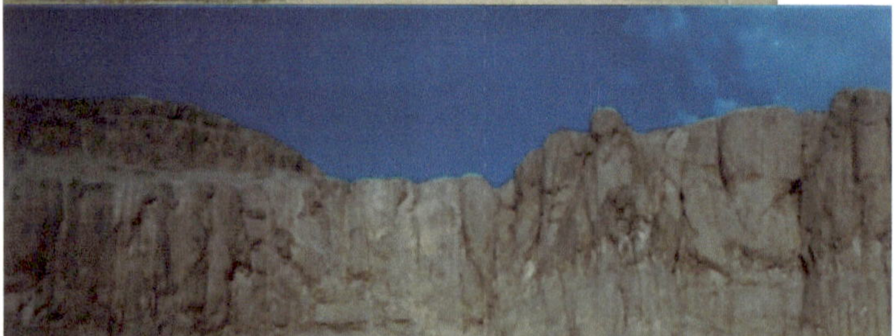

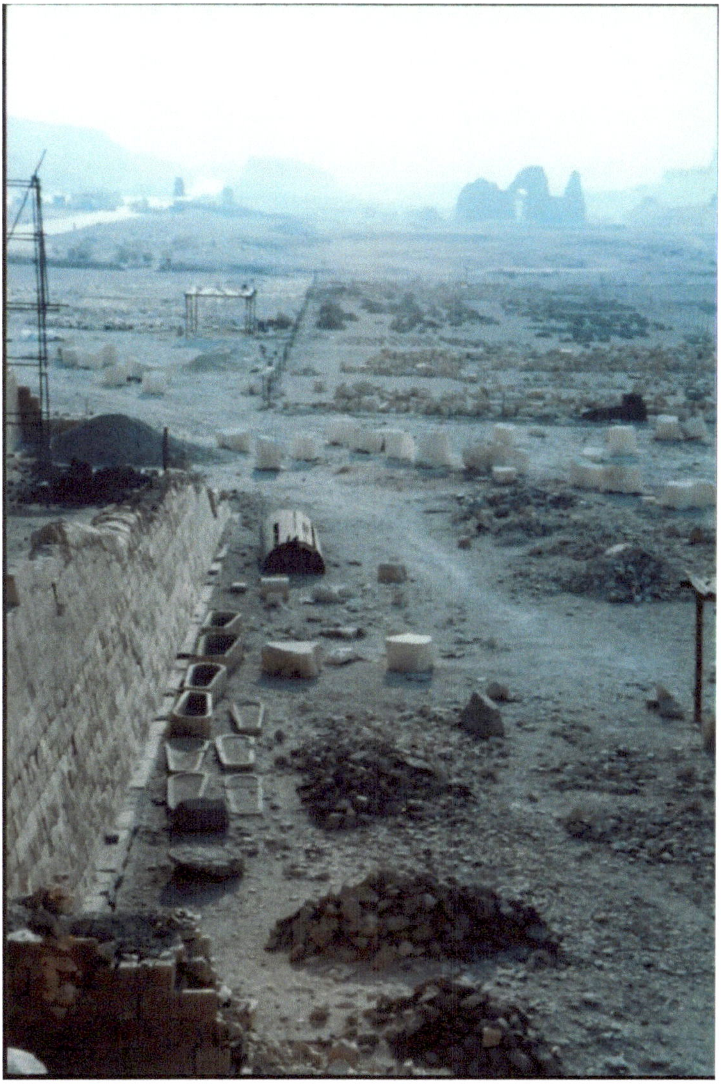

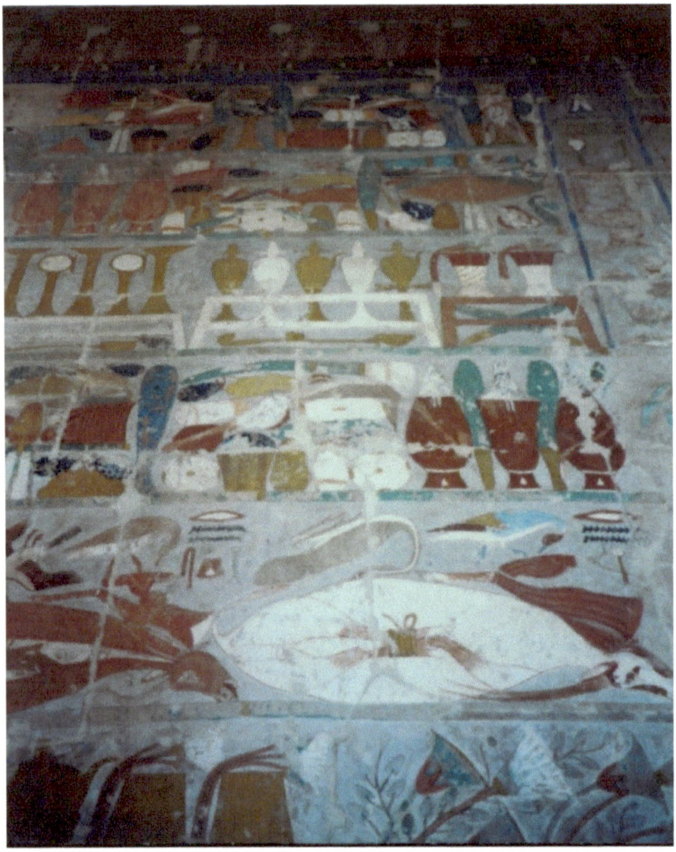

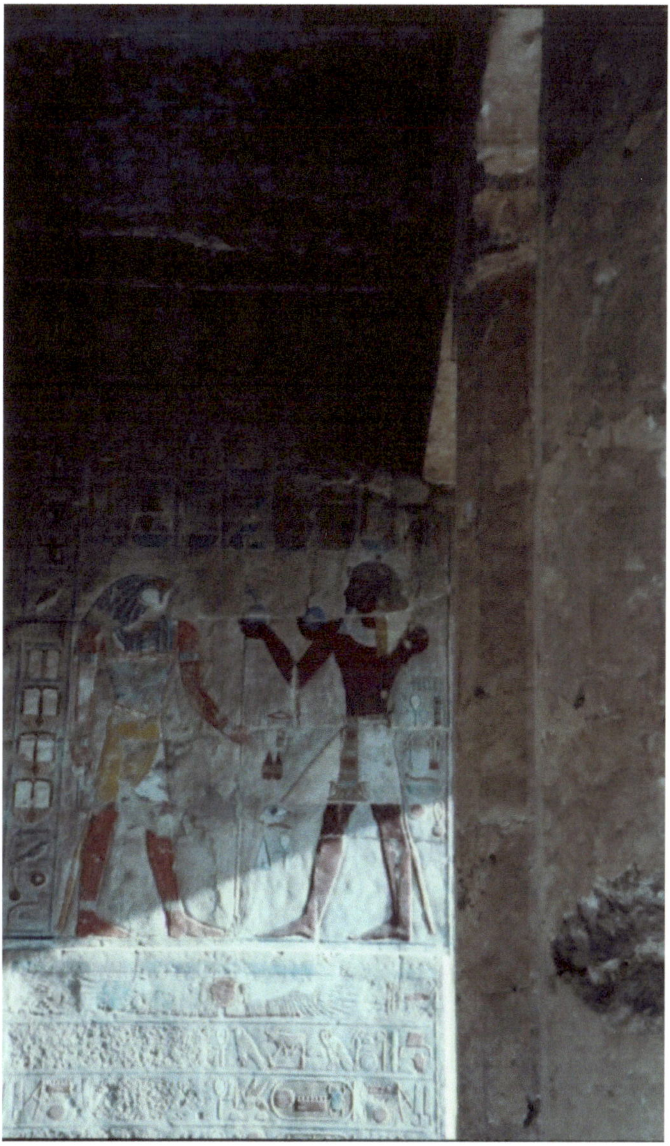

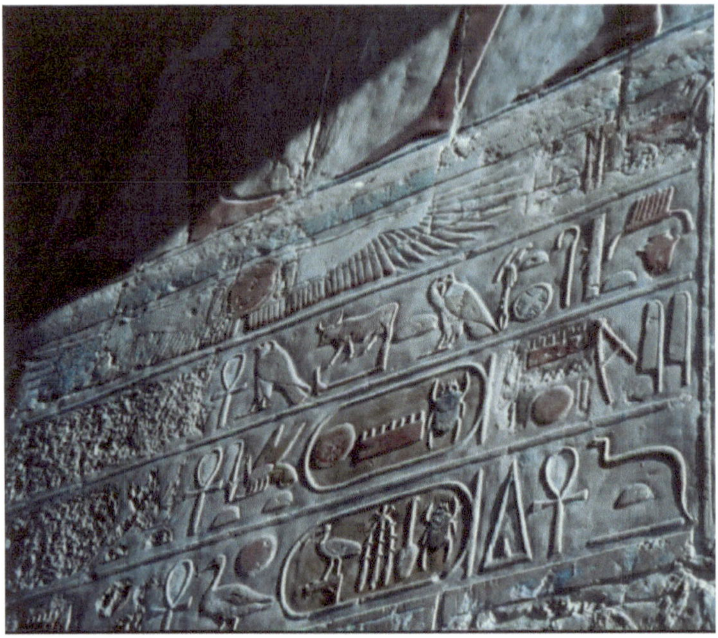

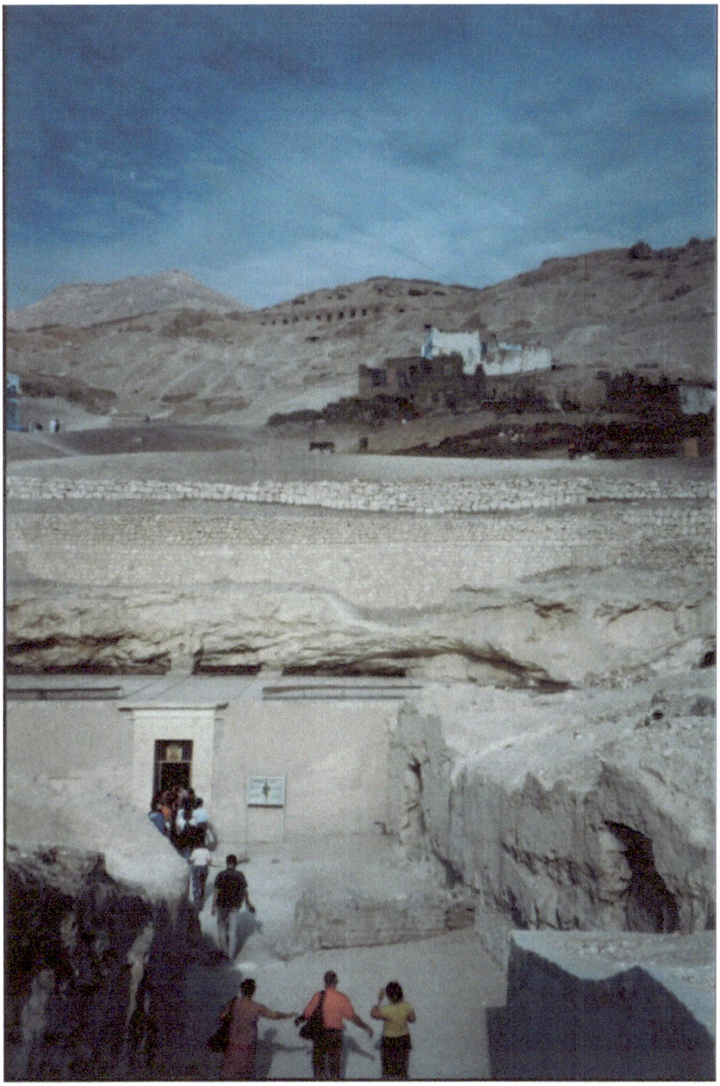

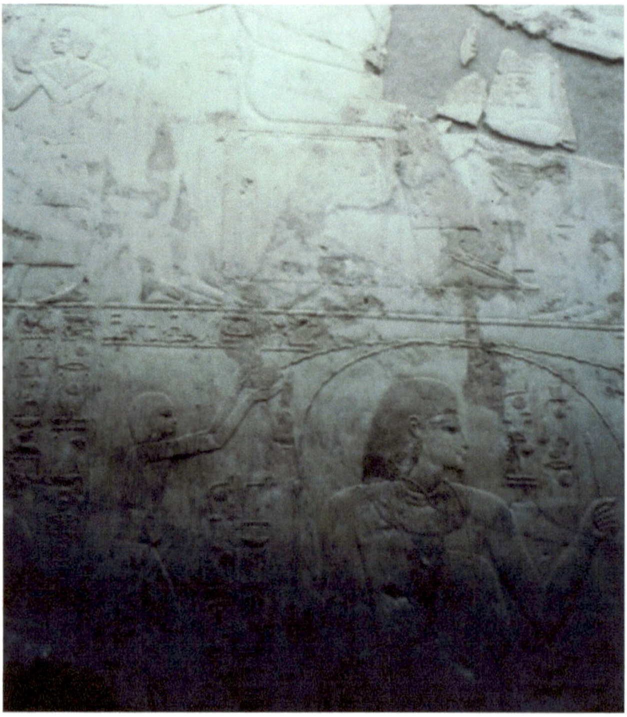

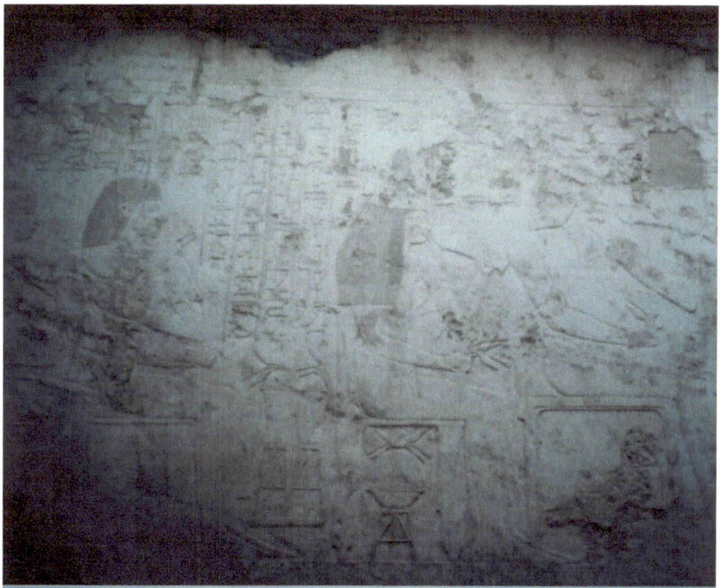
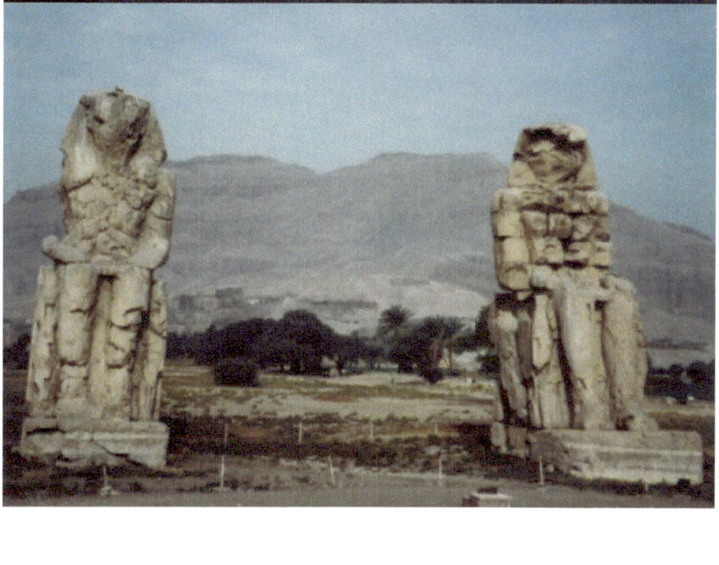

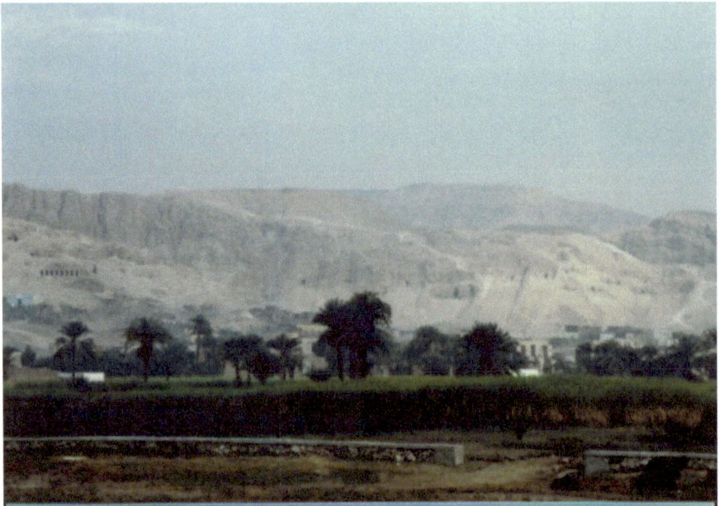
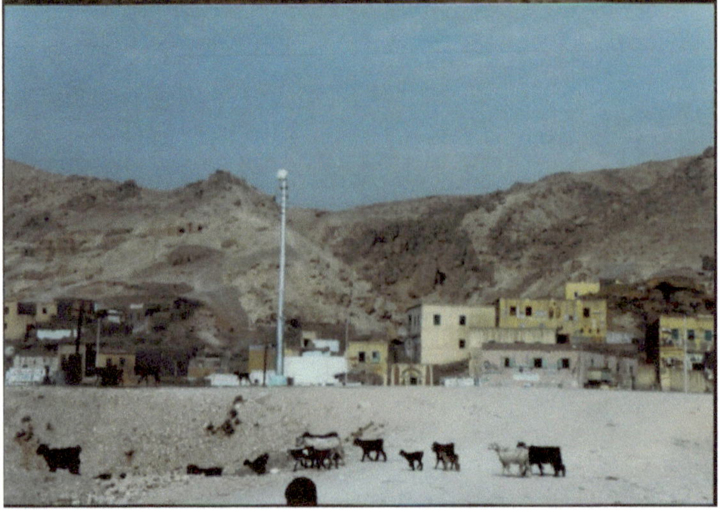

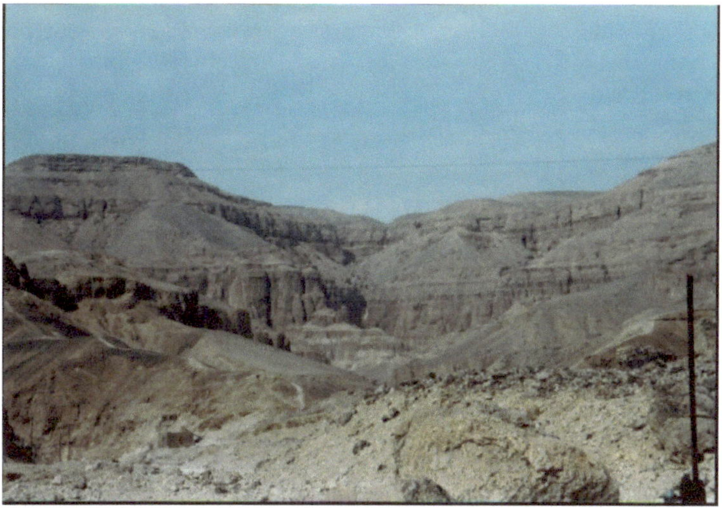

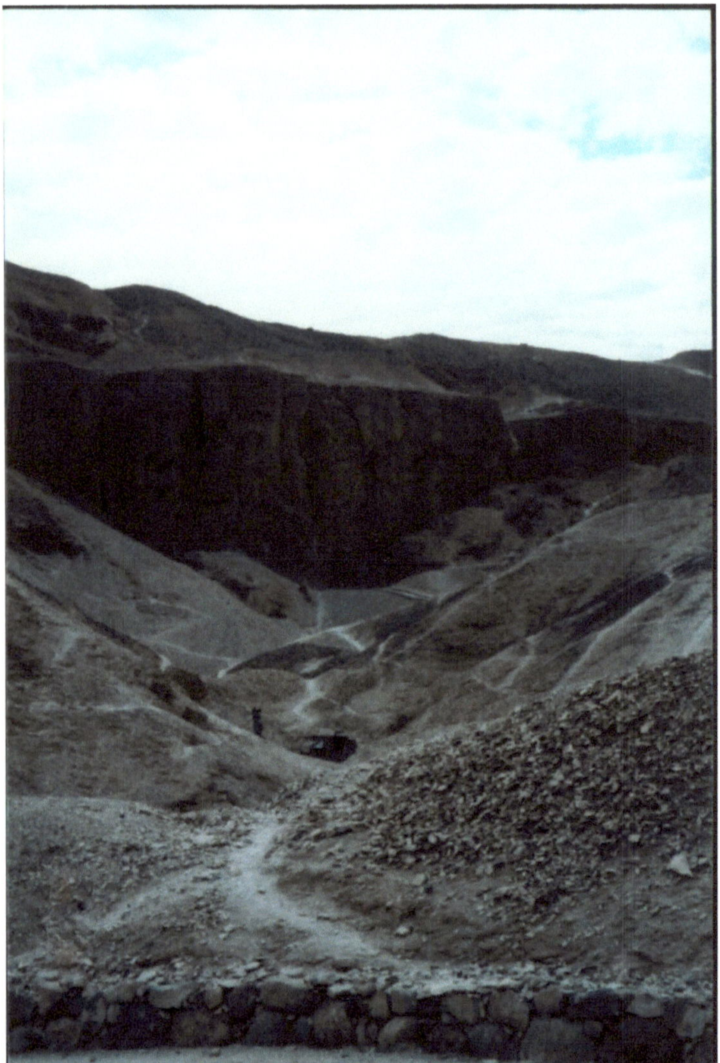

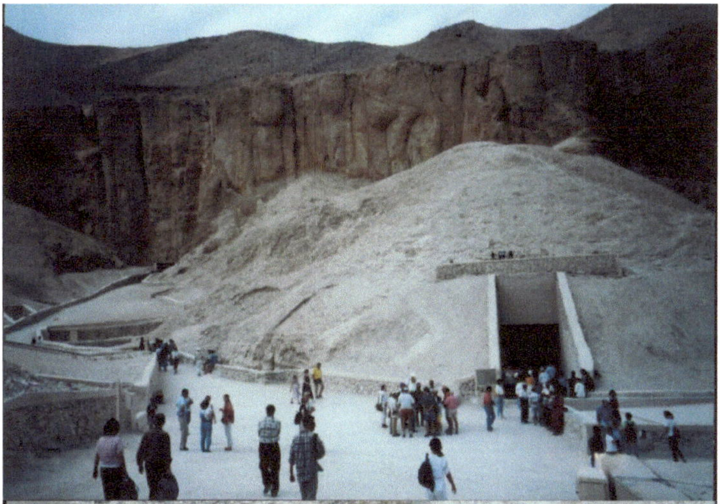

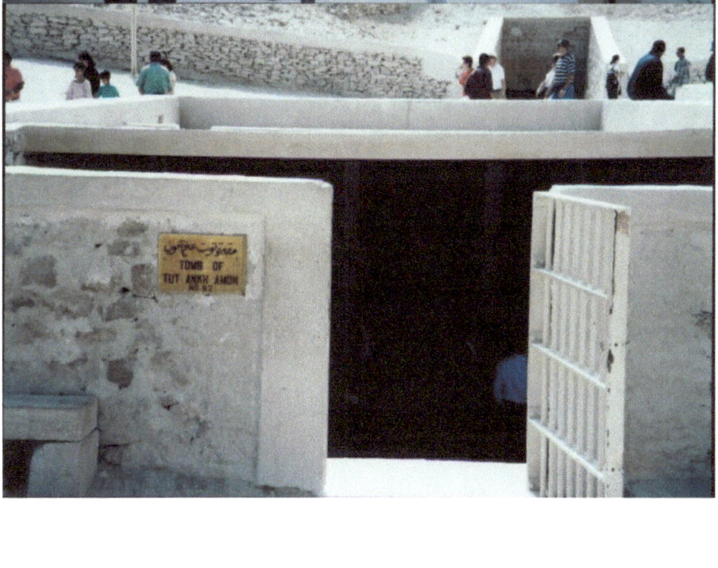
TOMB OF
TUT ANKH AMON

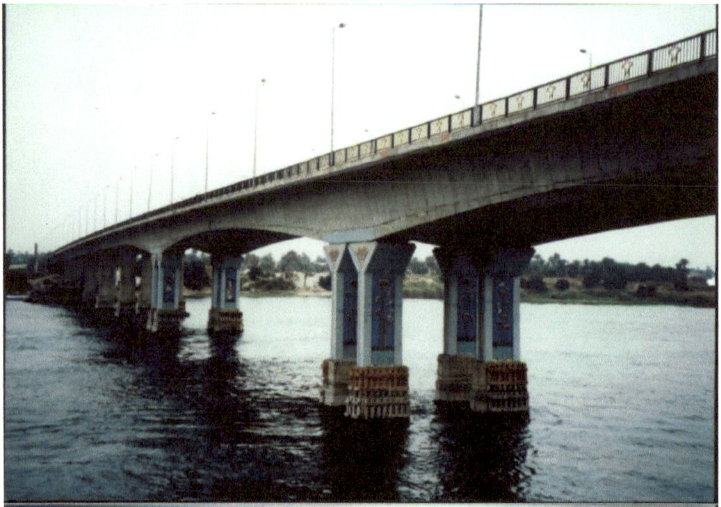

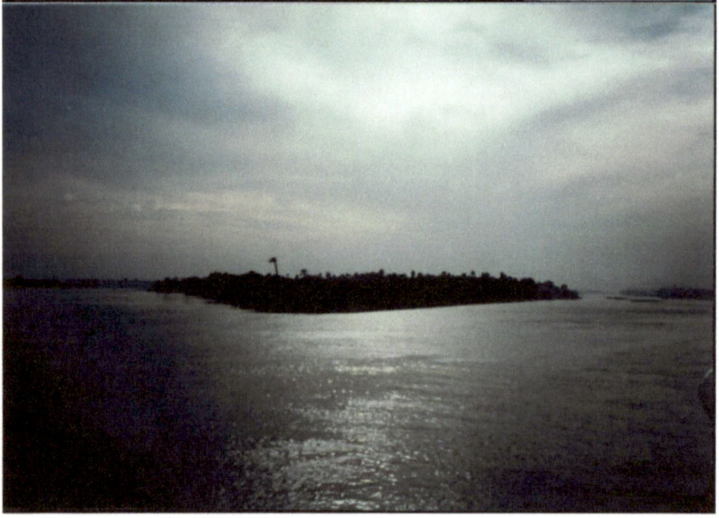

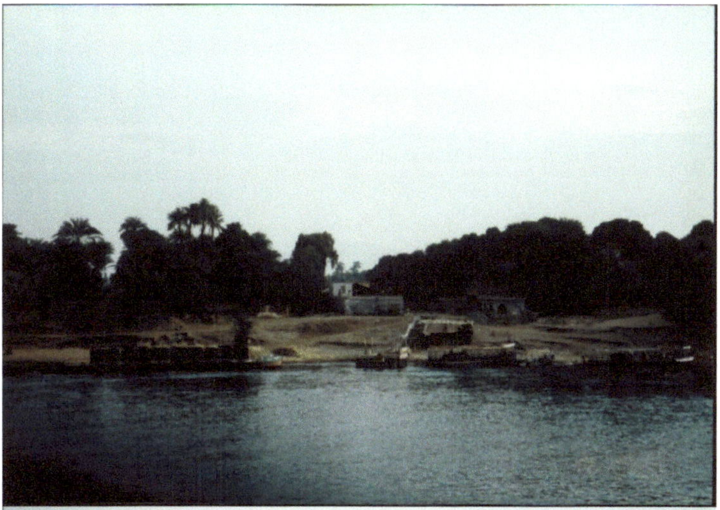

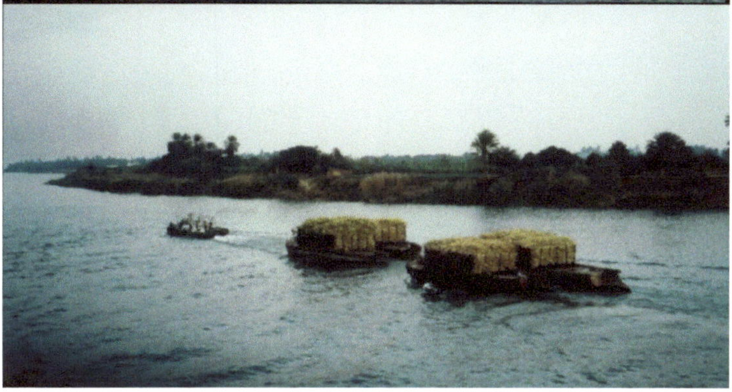

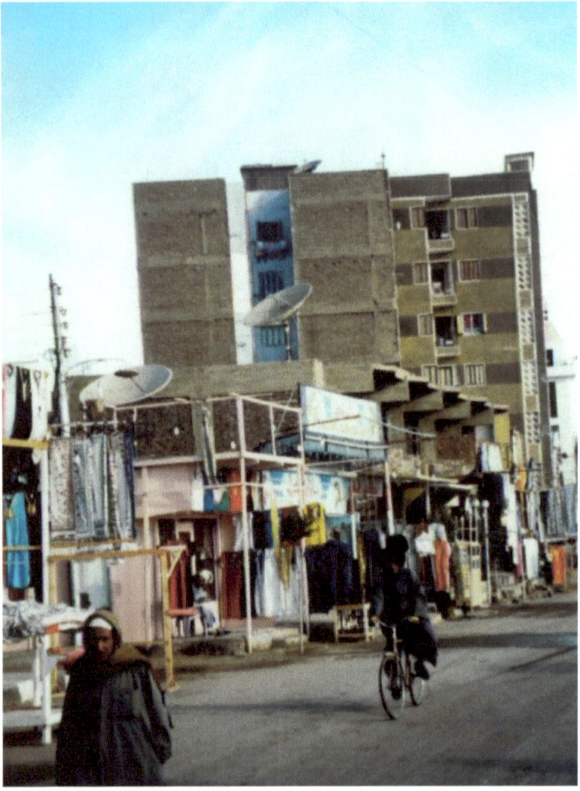

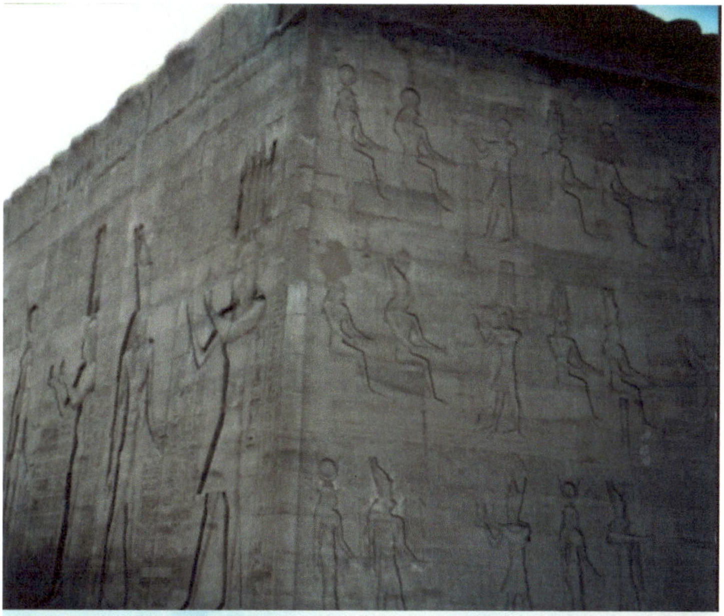

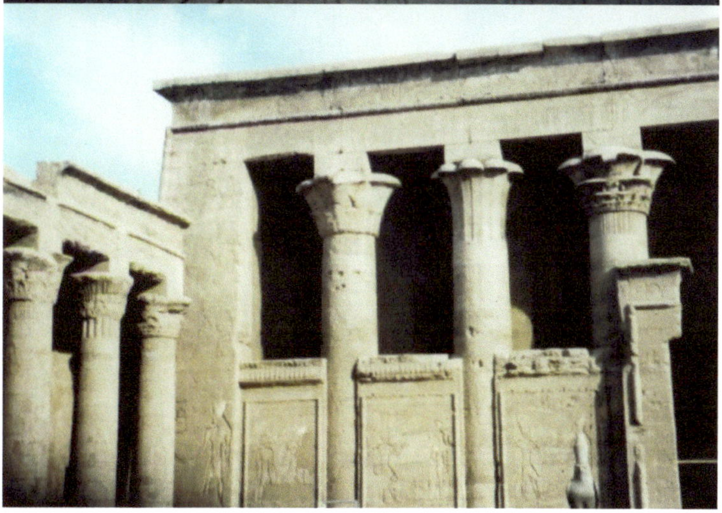

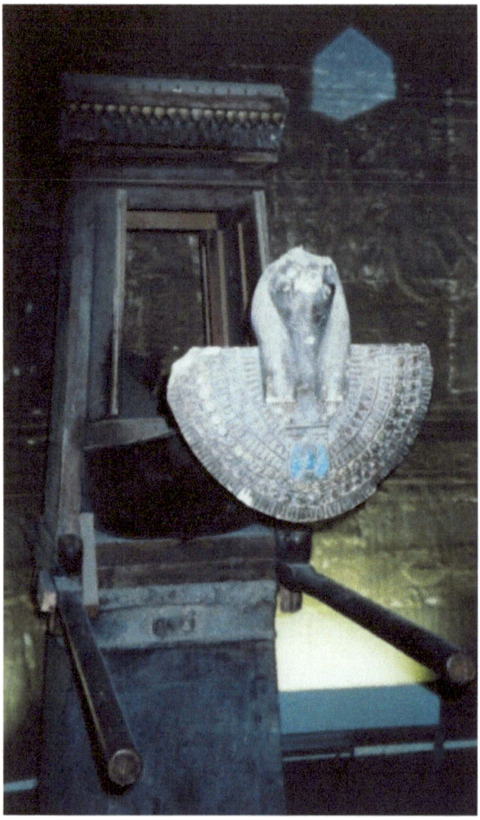

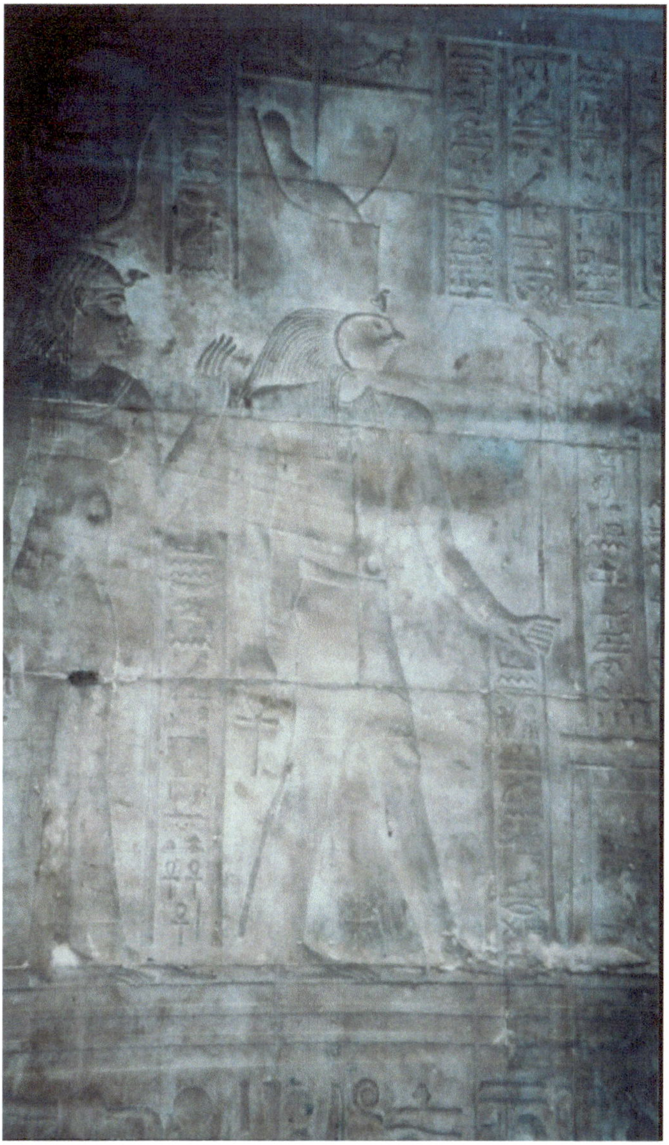

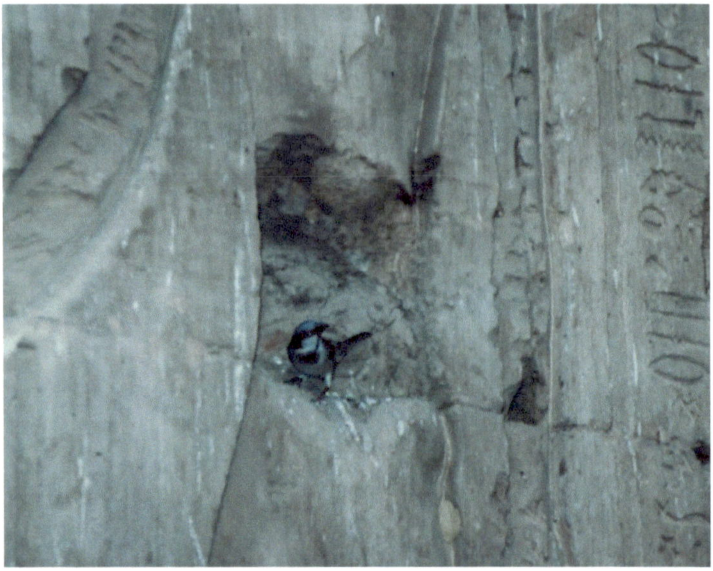

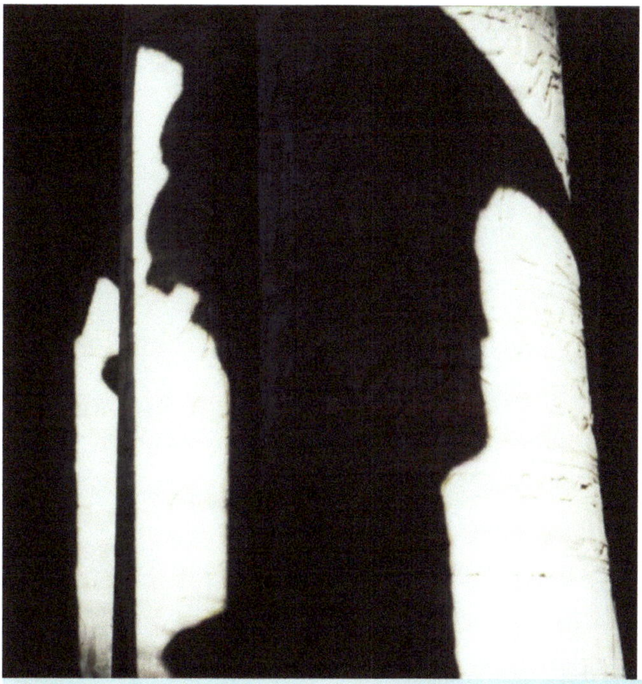
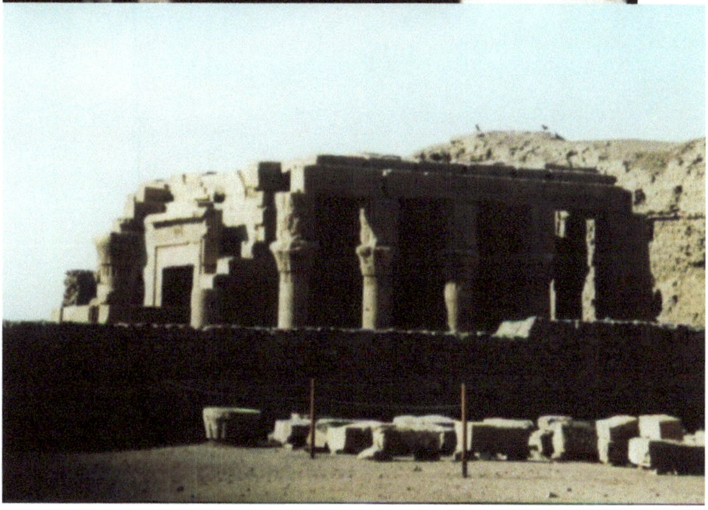

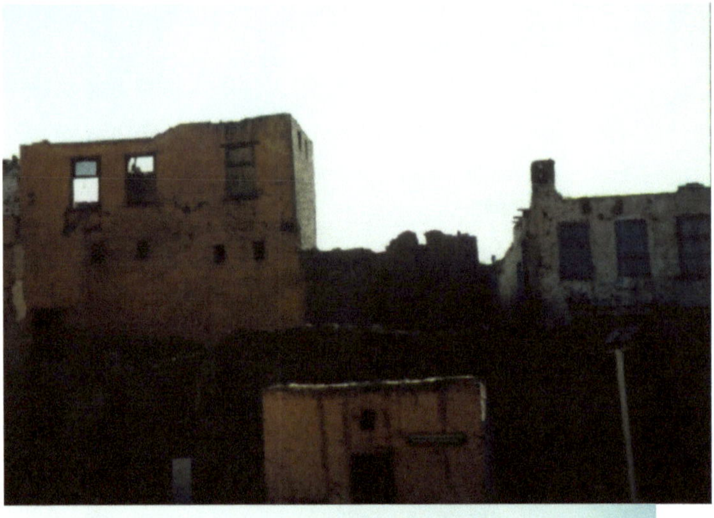

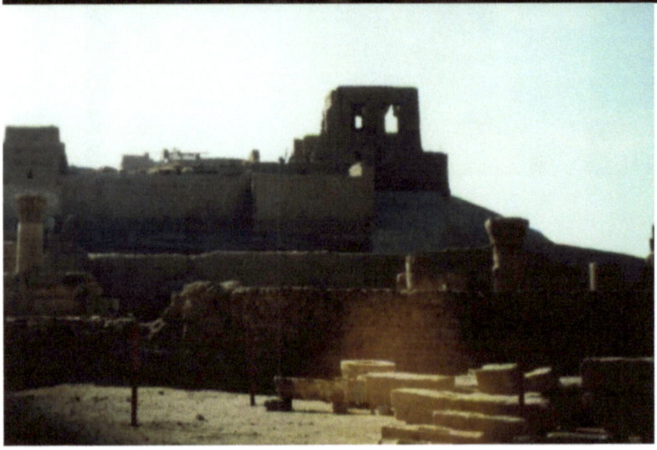

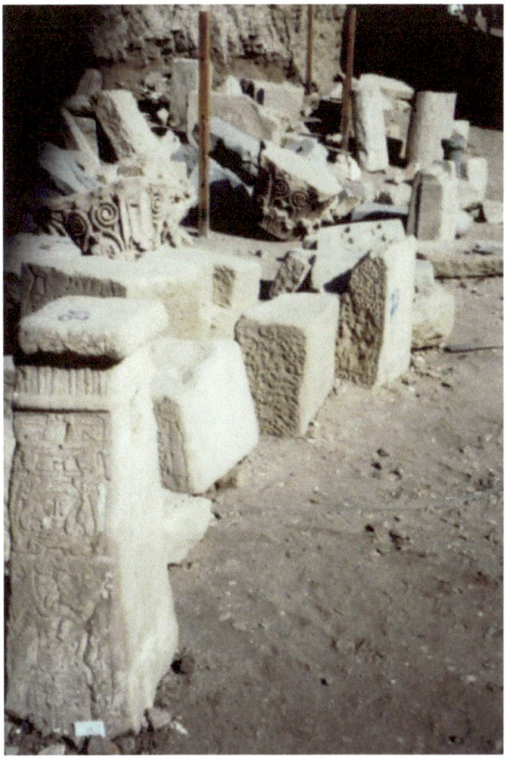

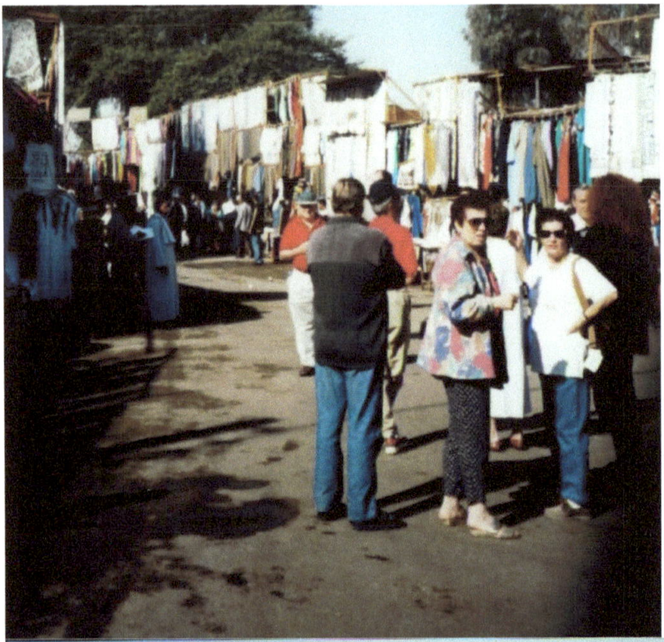

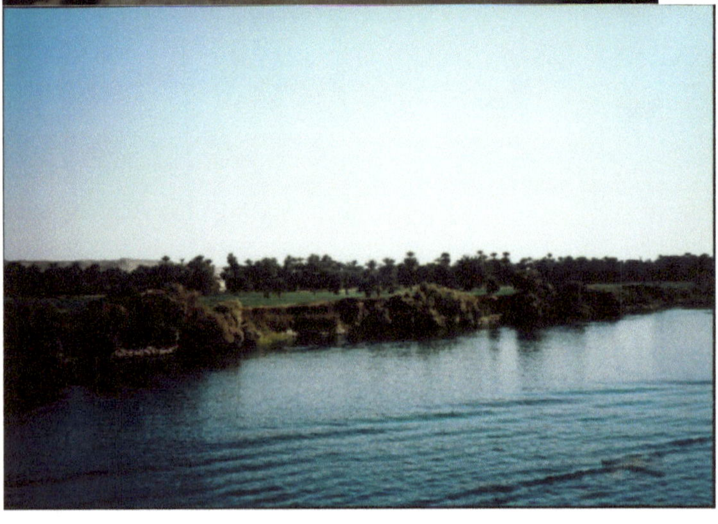

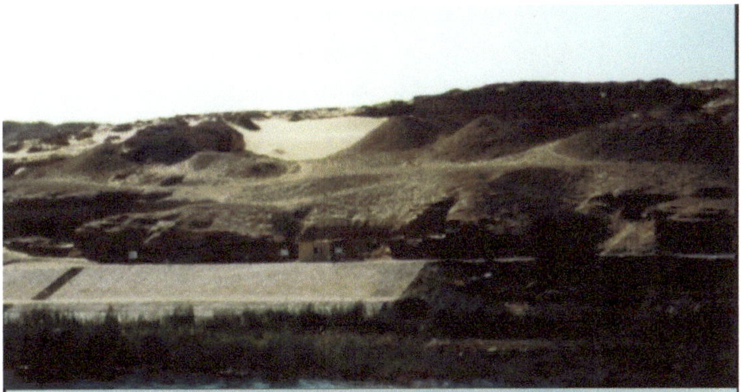

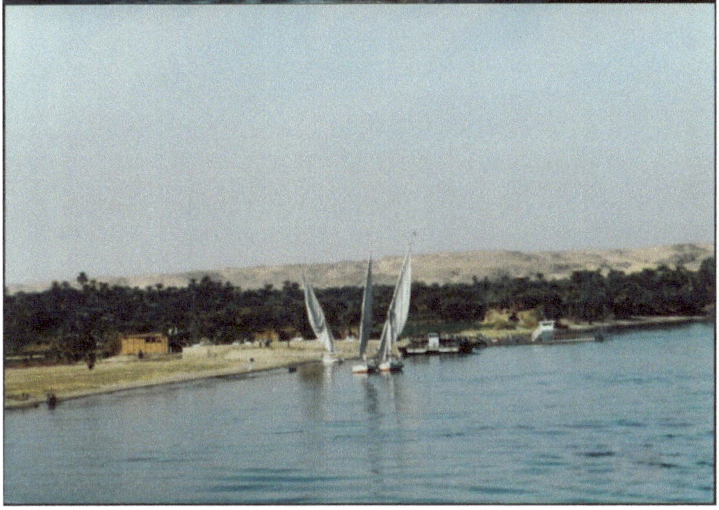

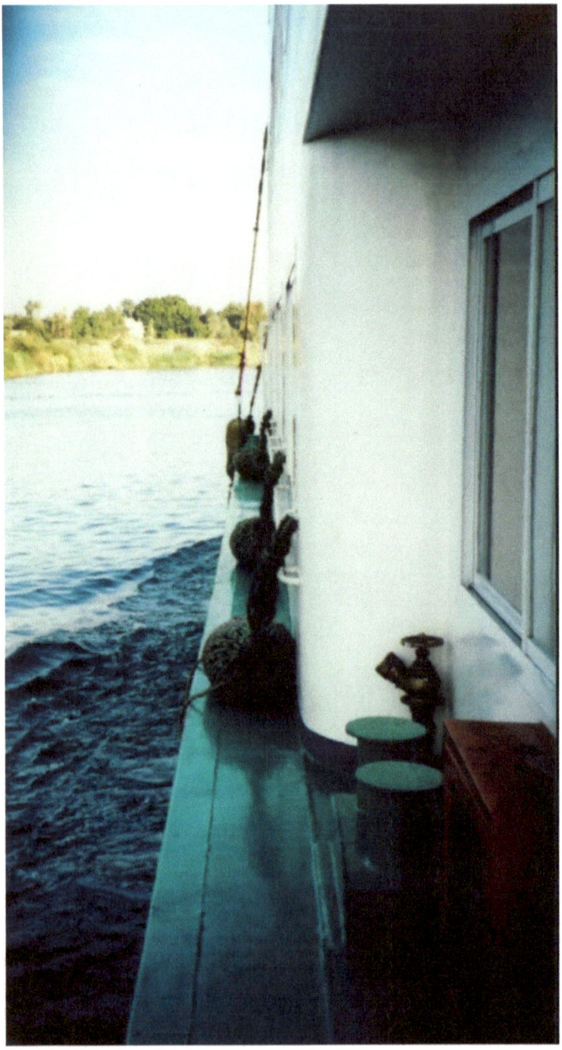

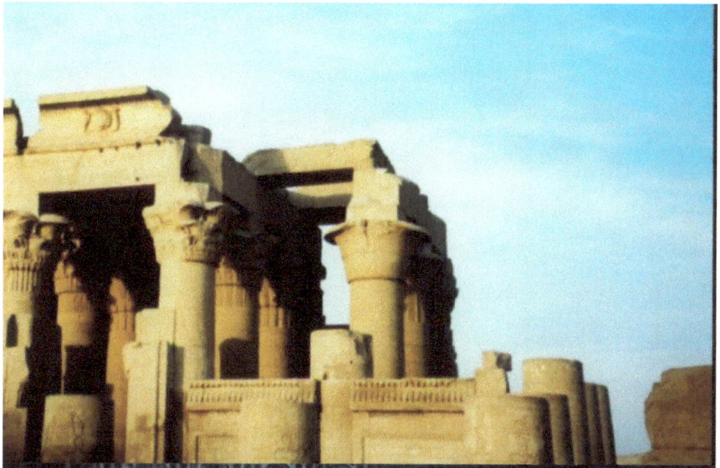

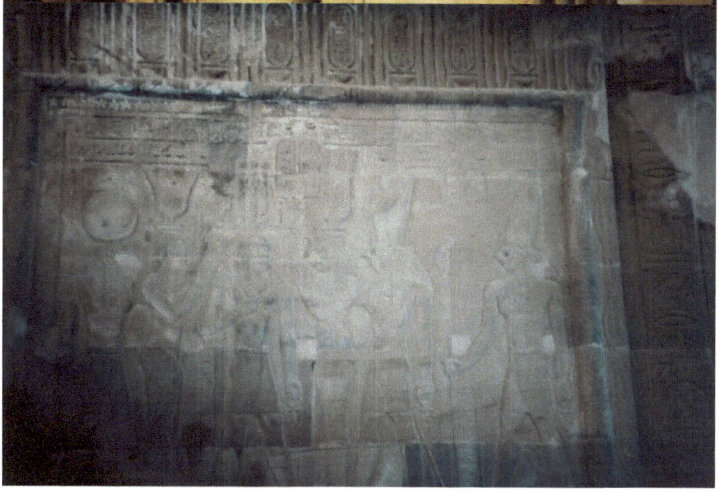

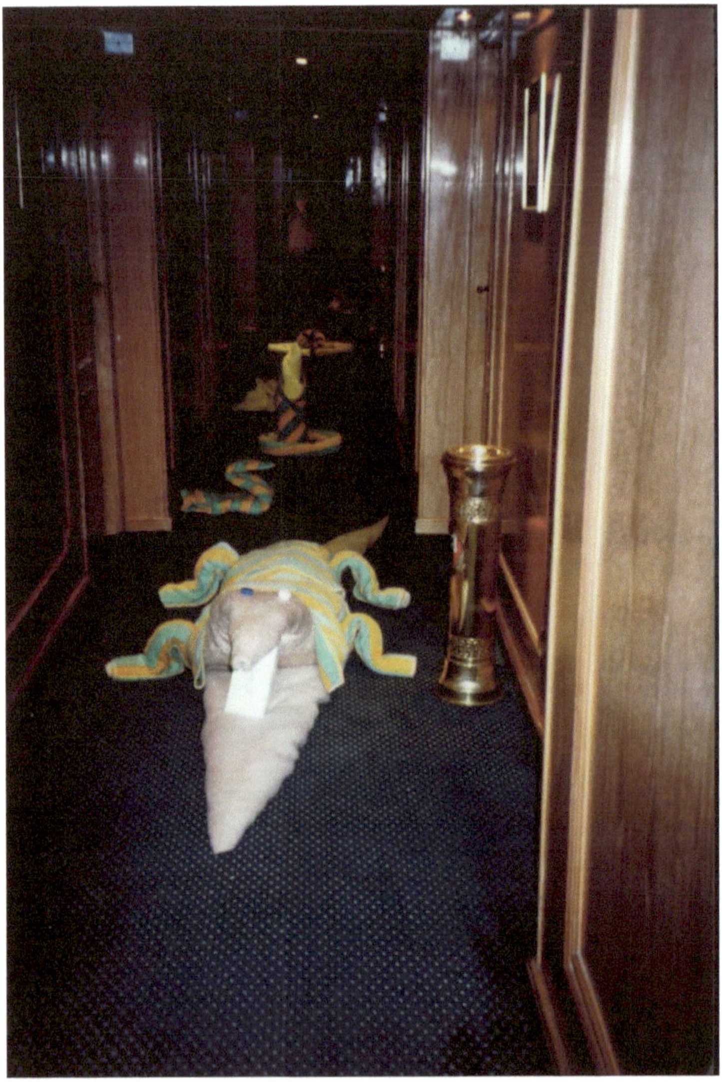

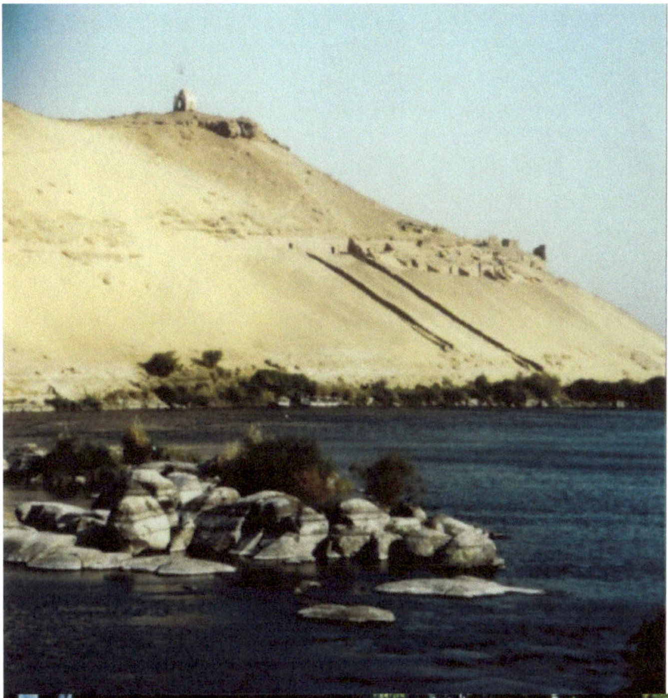

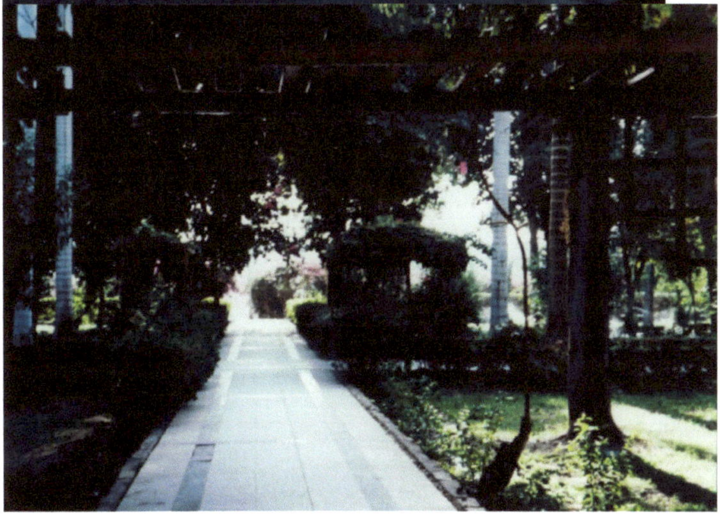

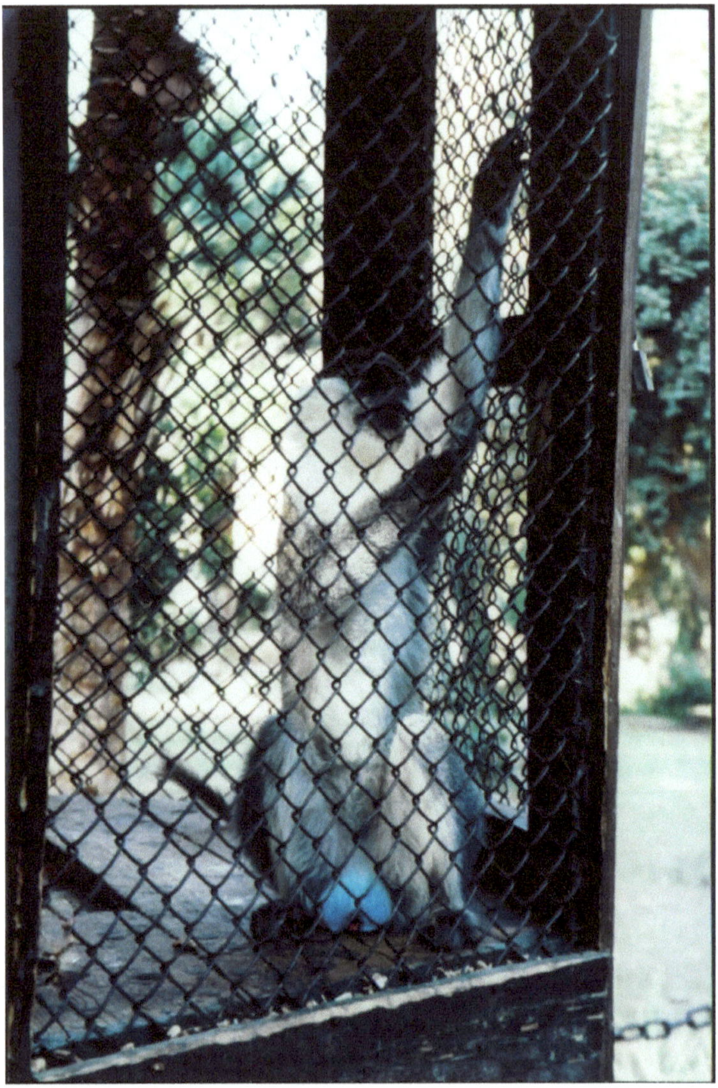

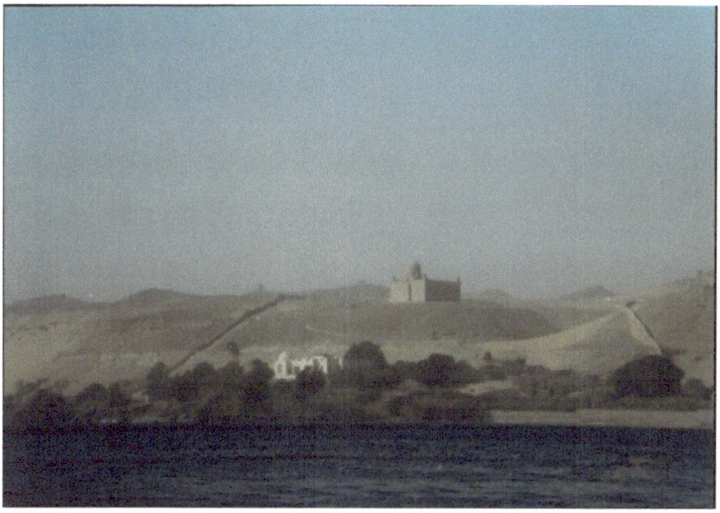

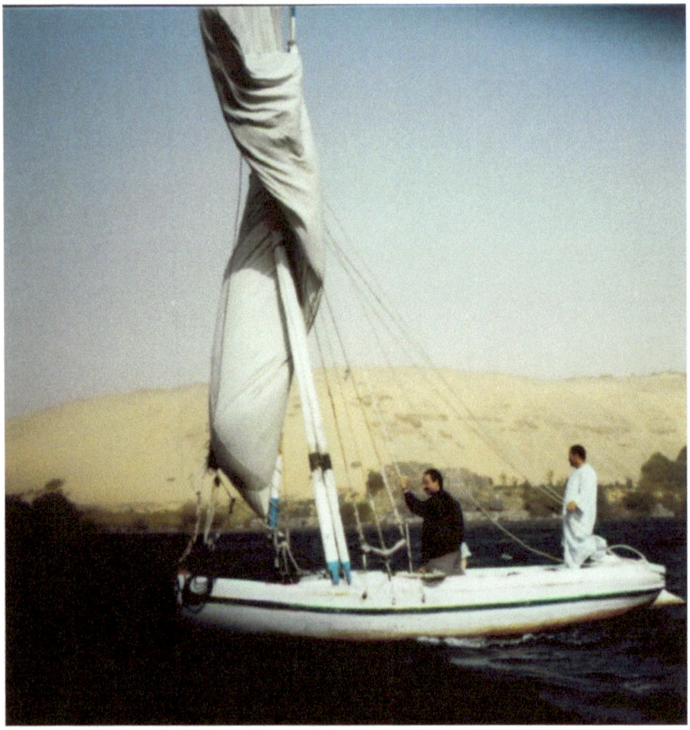

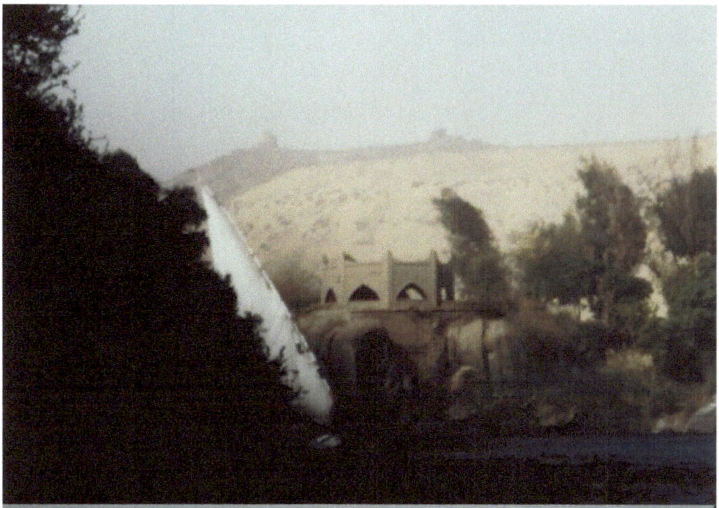

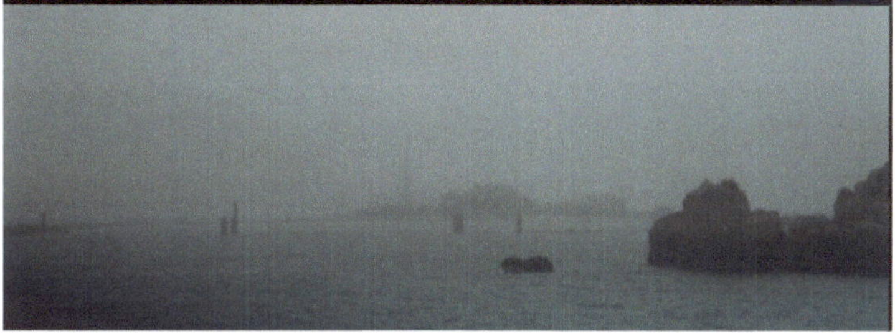

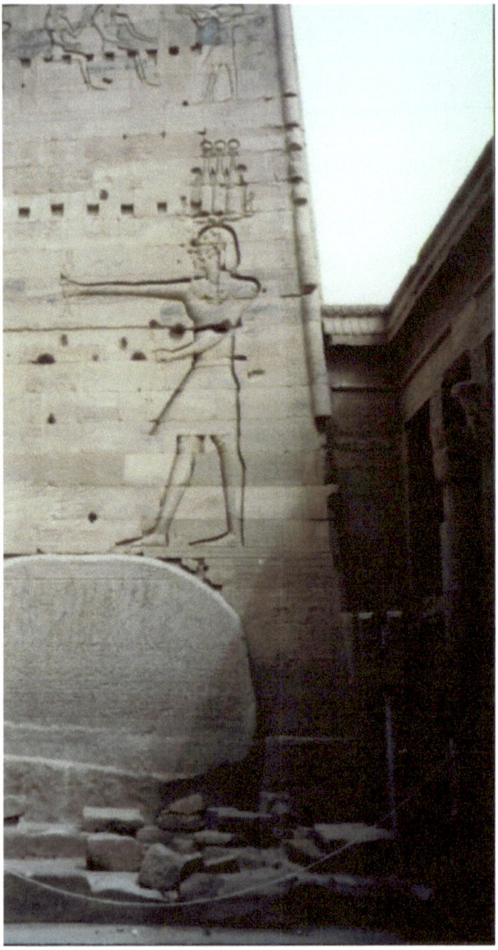

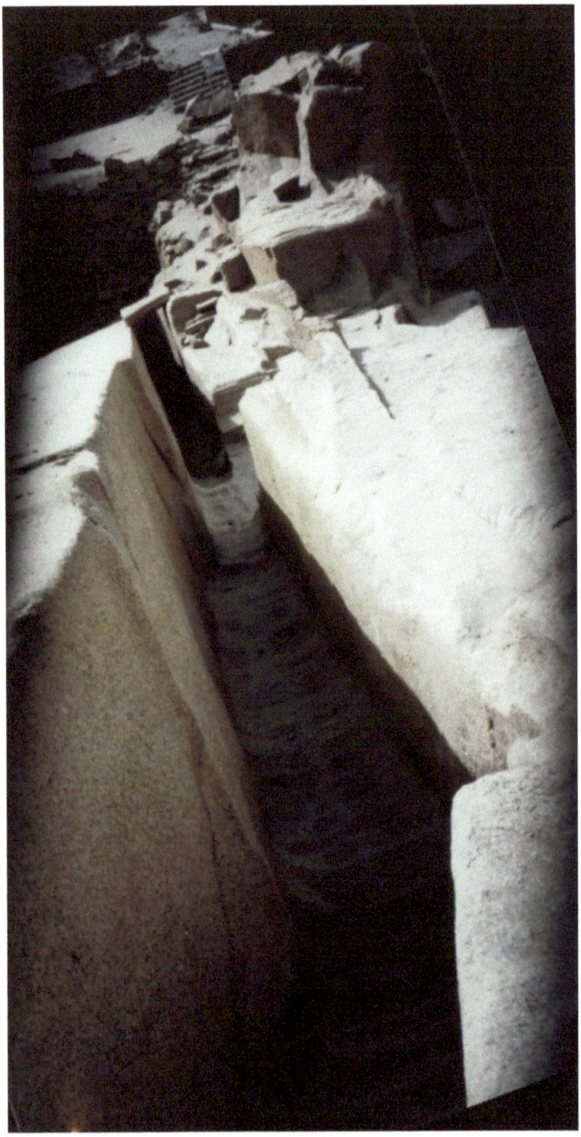

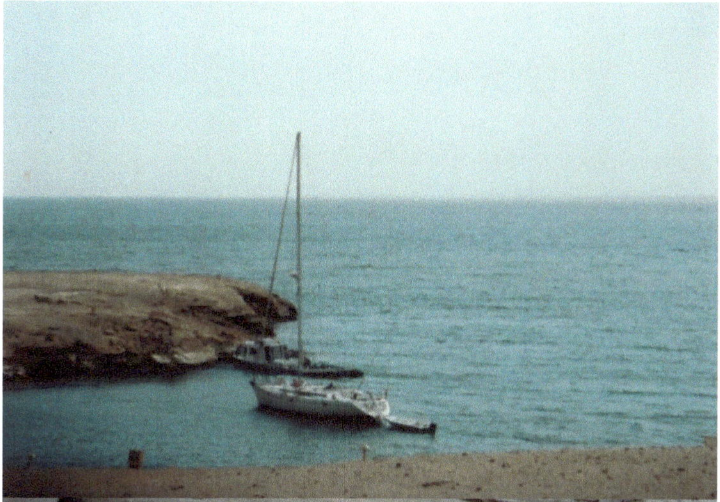

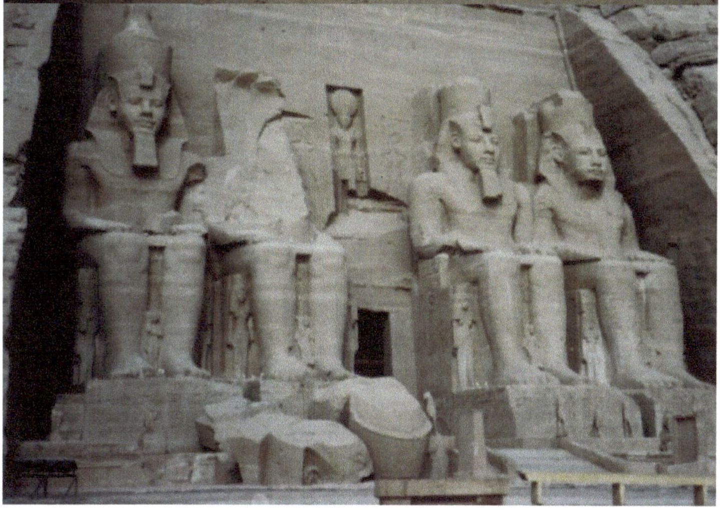

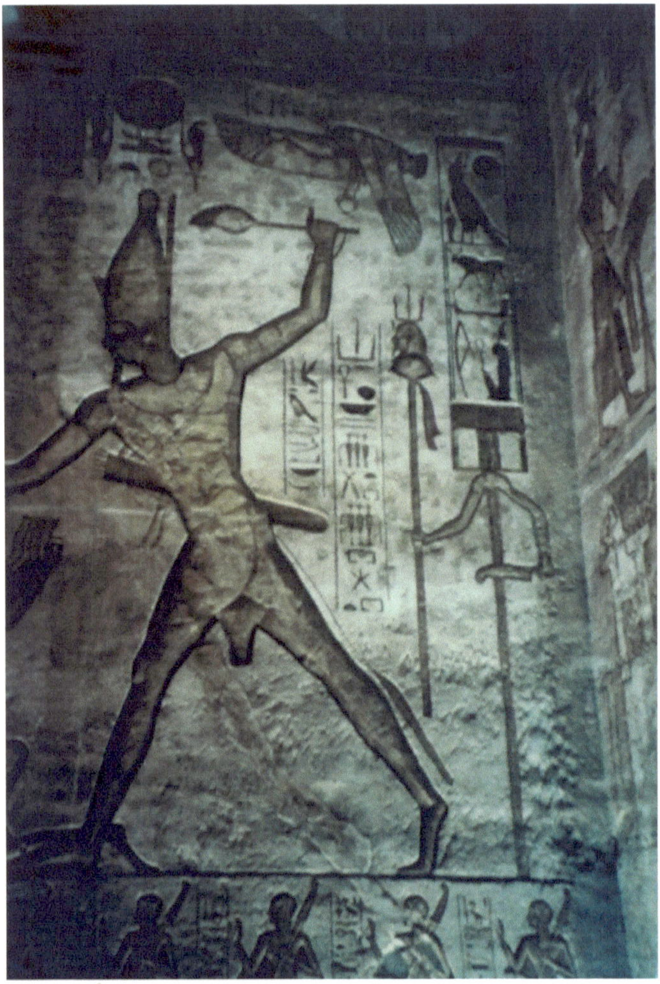

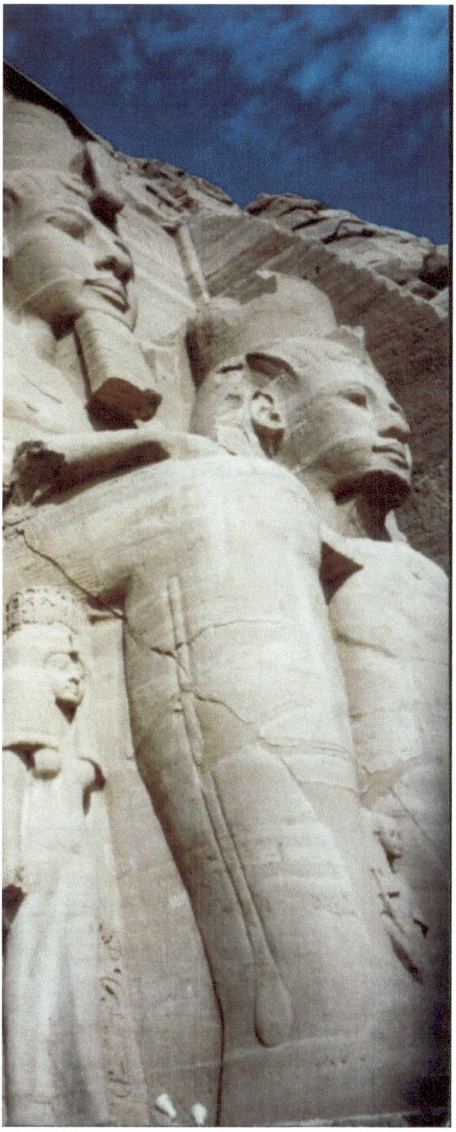

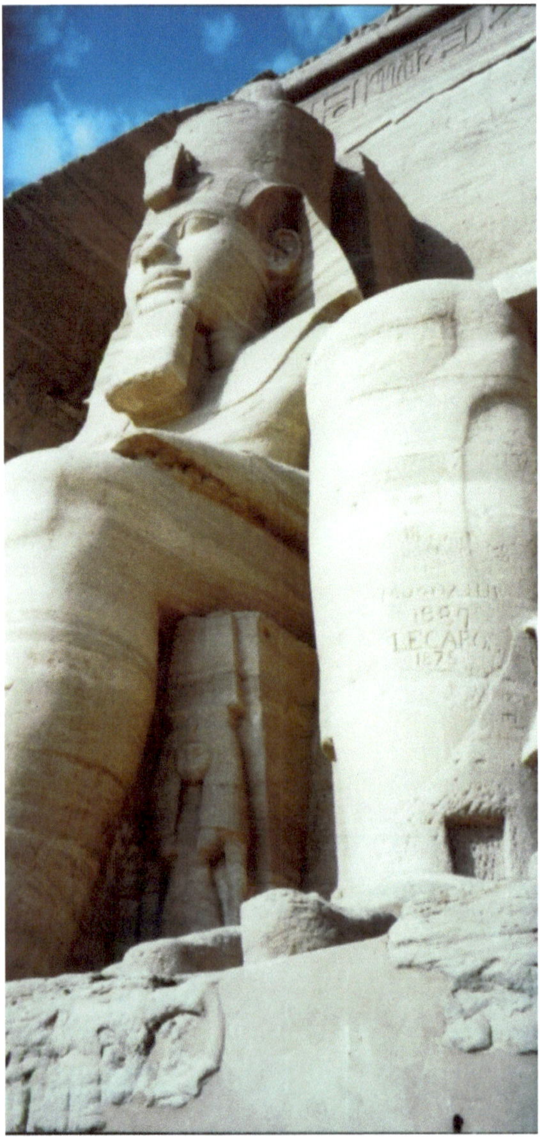

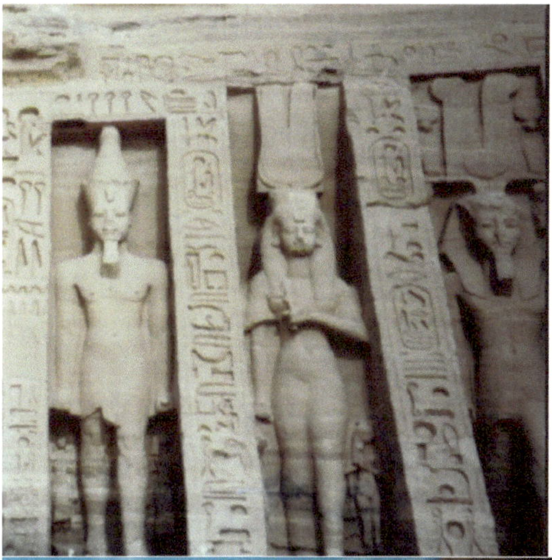

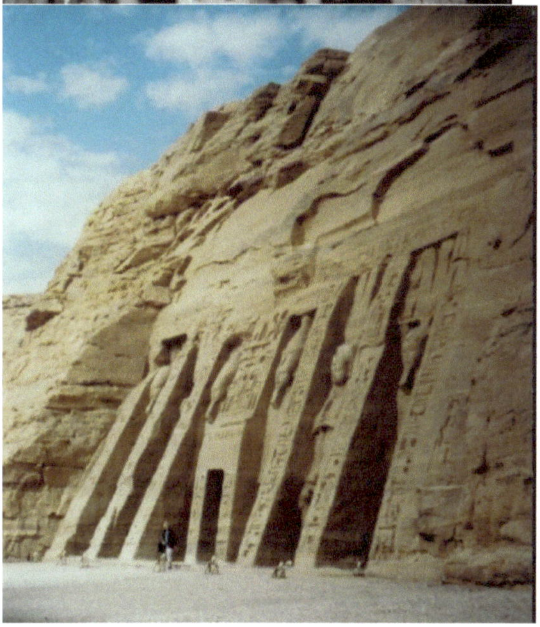

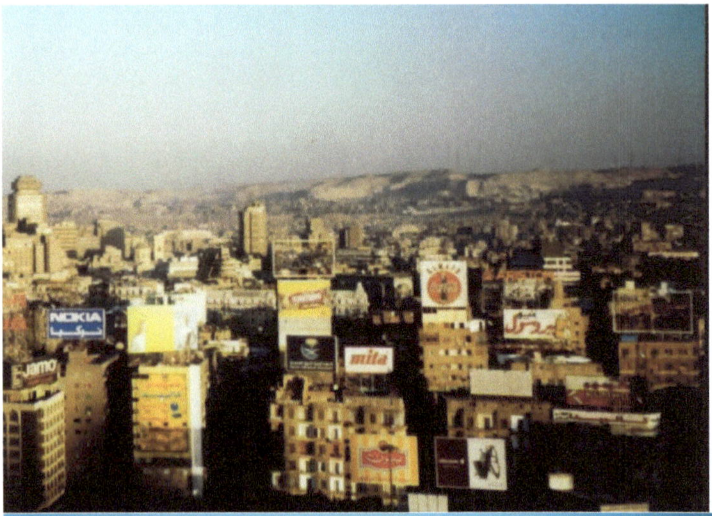
NOKIA
mita

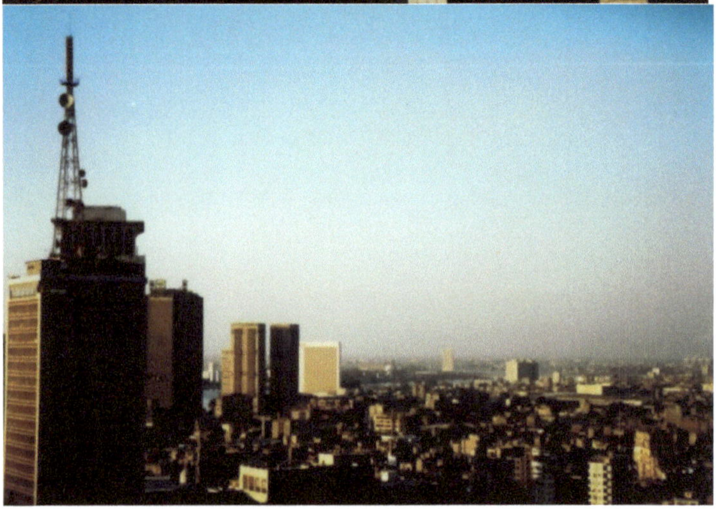

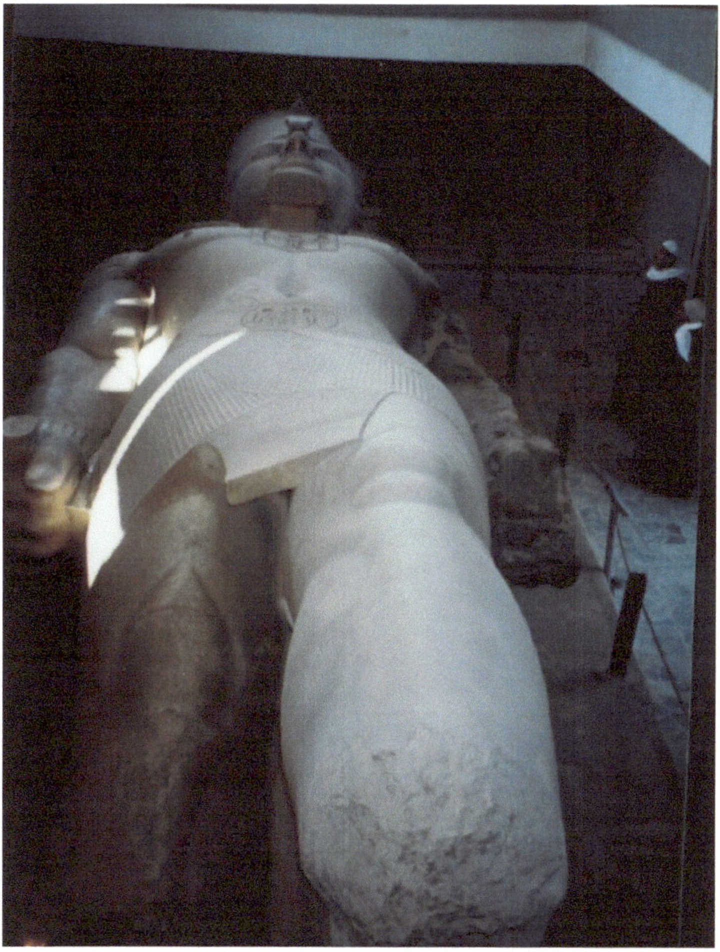

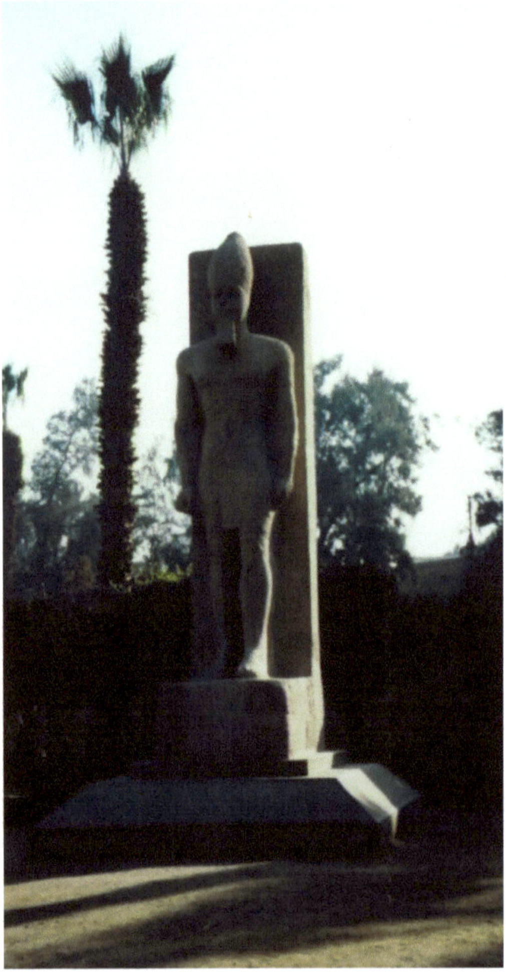

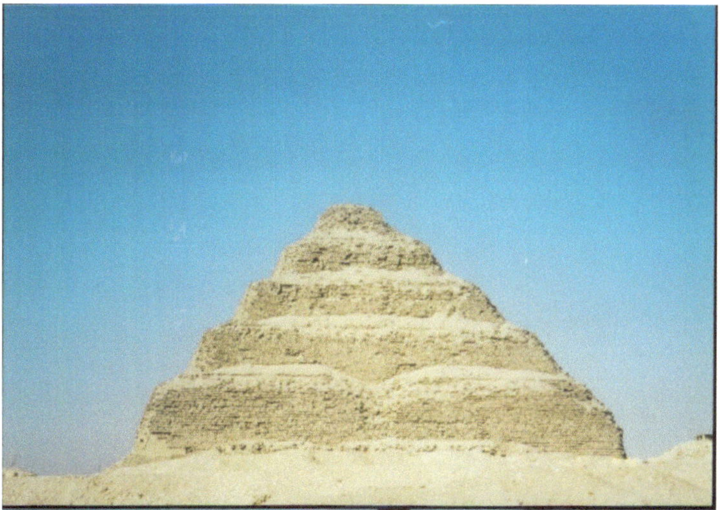

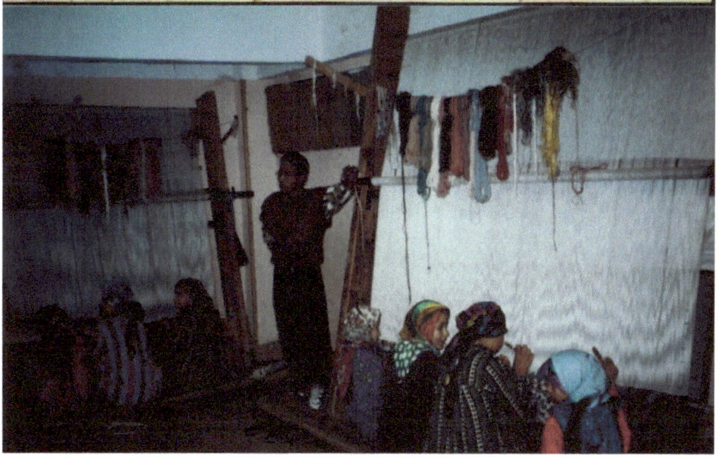

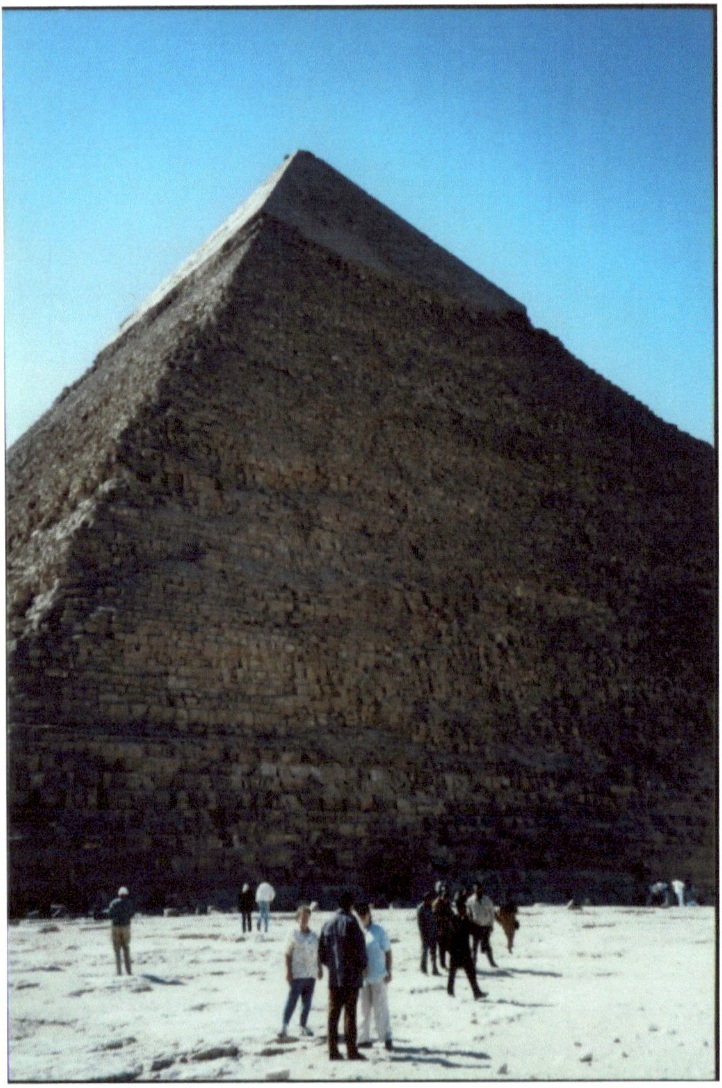

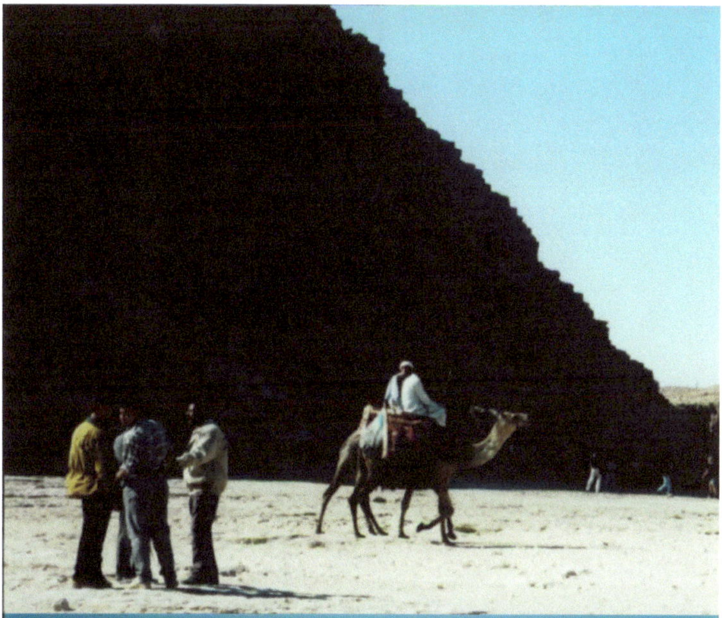

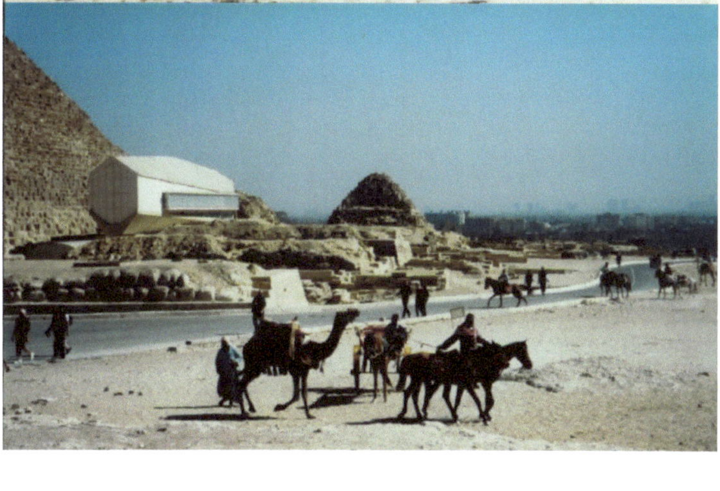

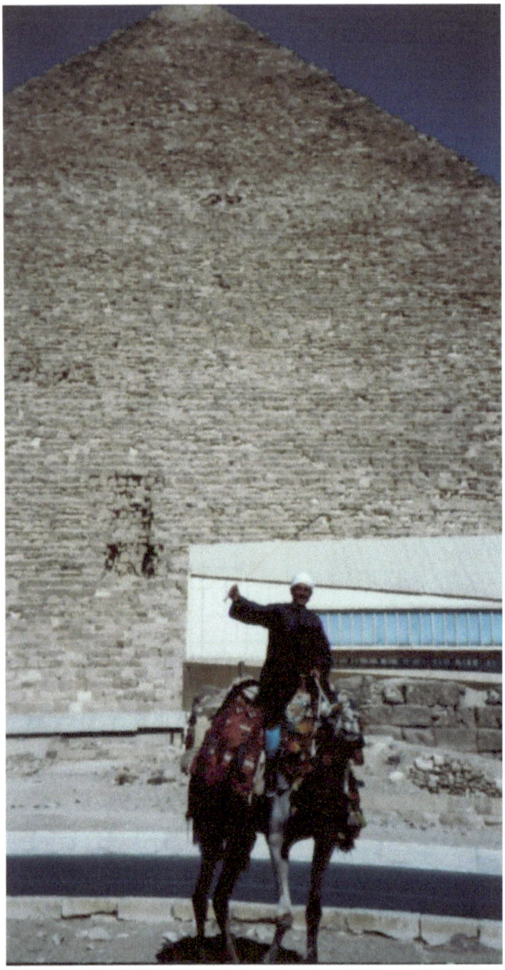

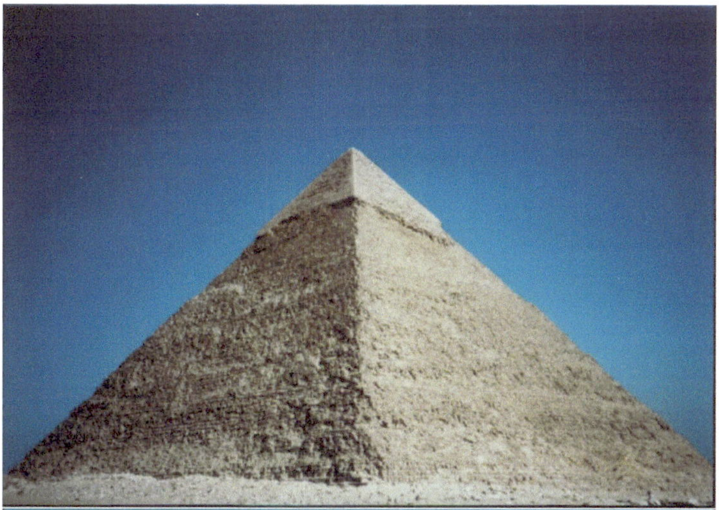

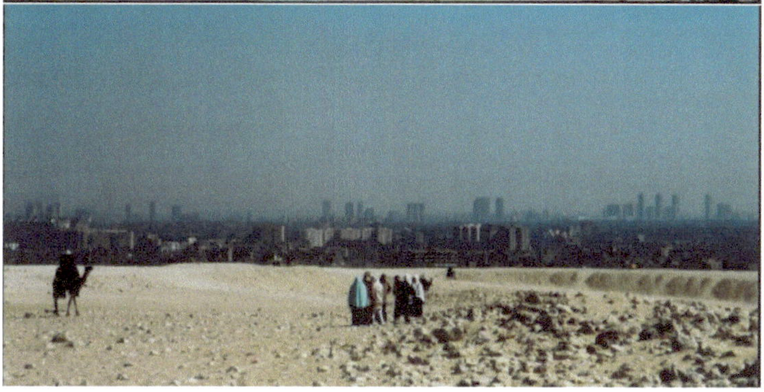

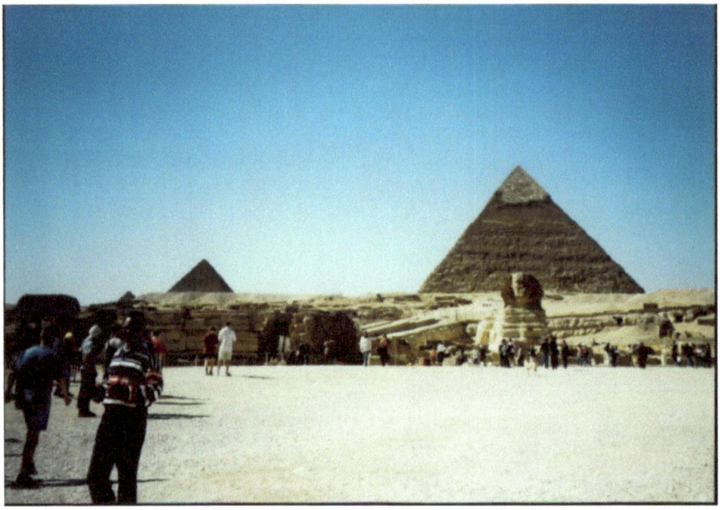

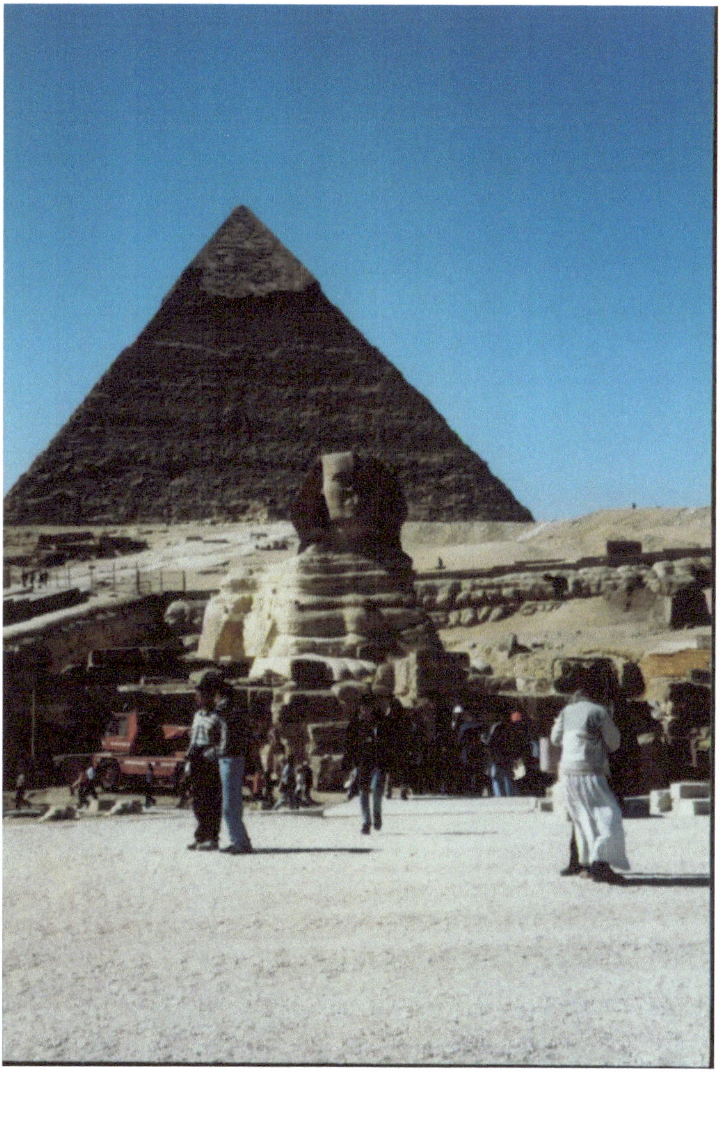

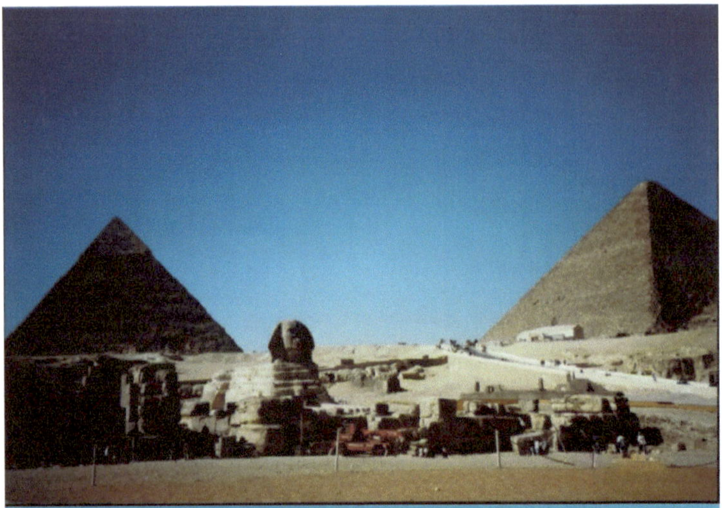

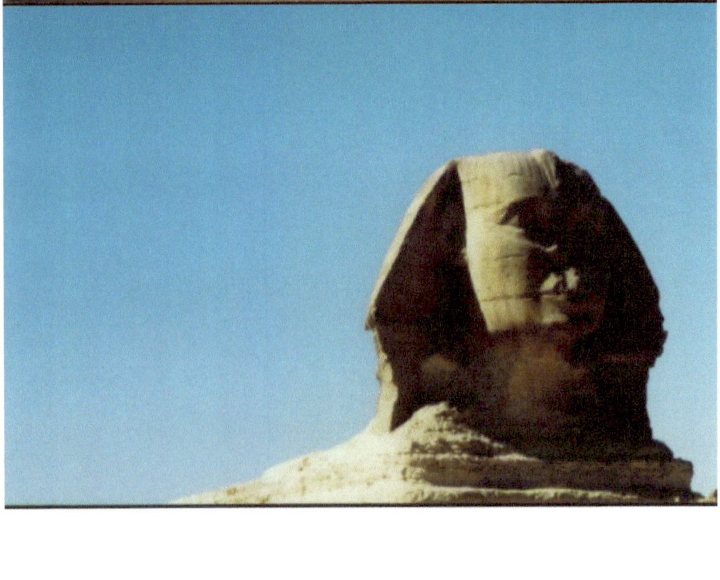

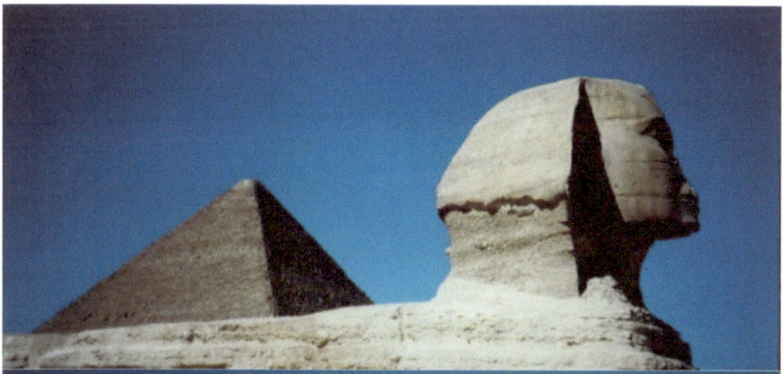

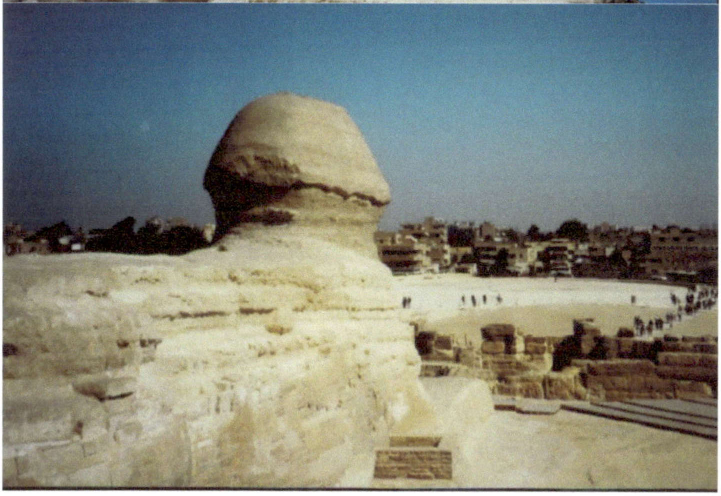

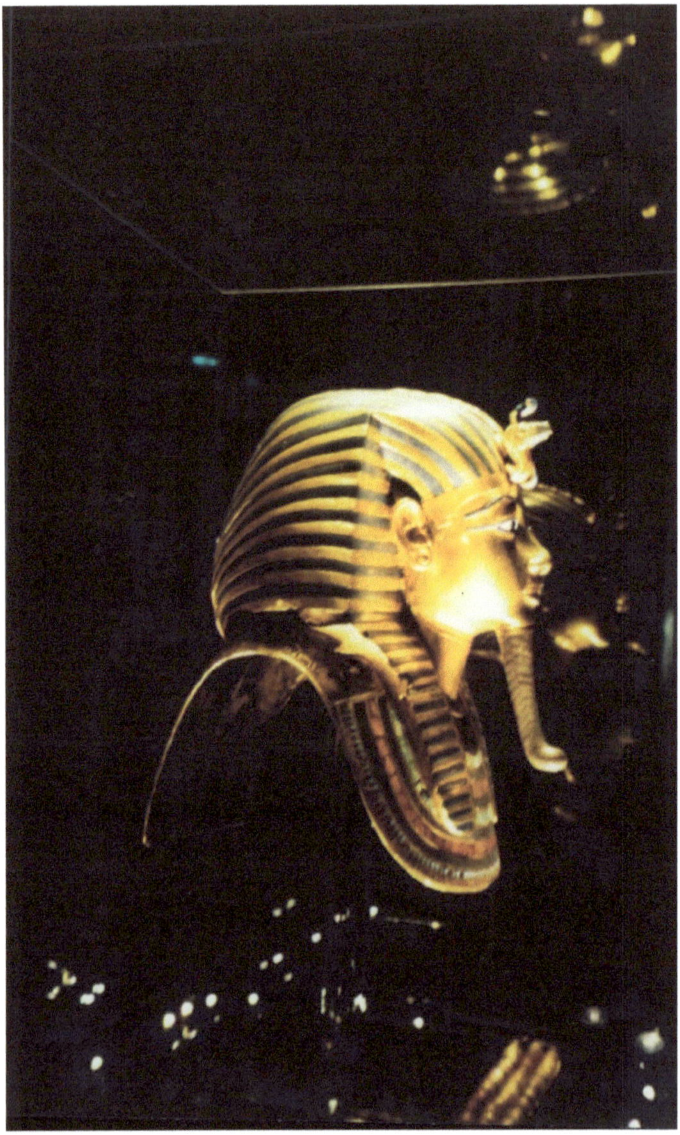

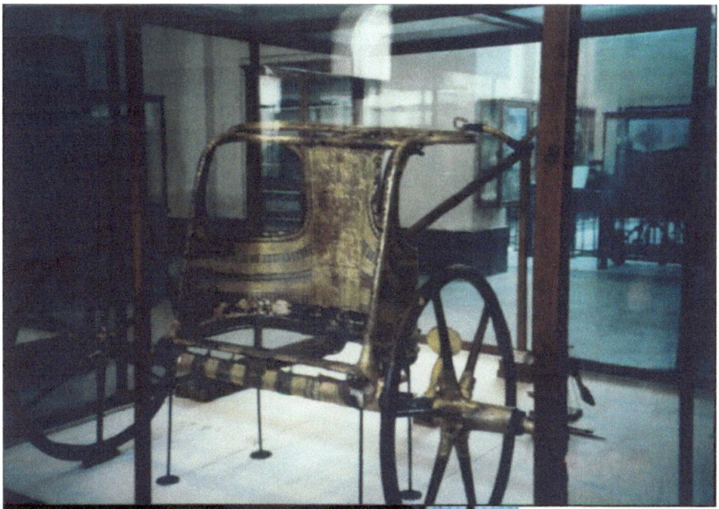

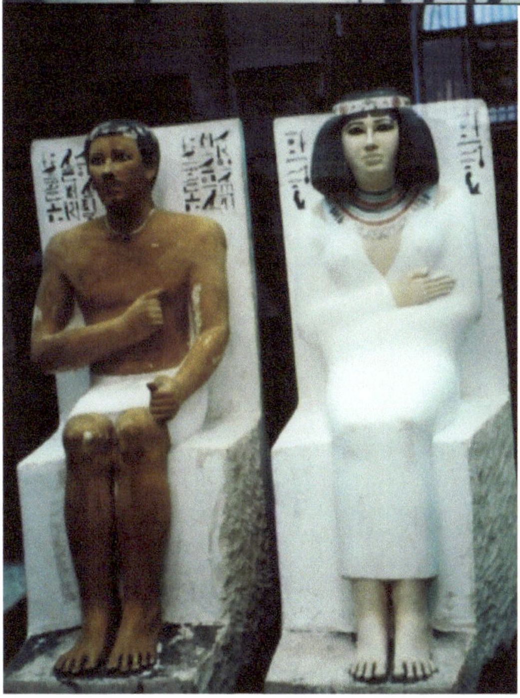

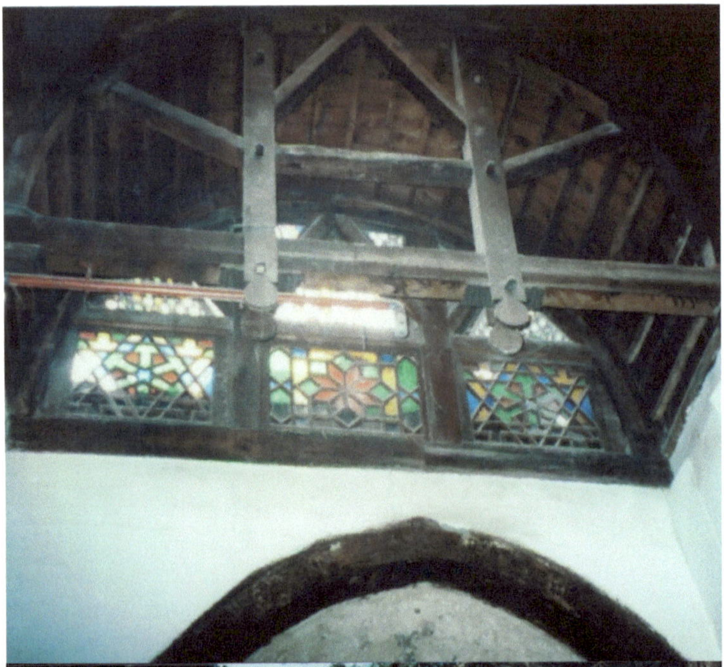
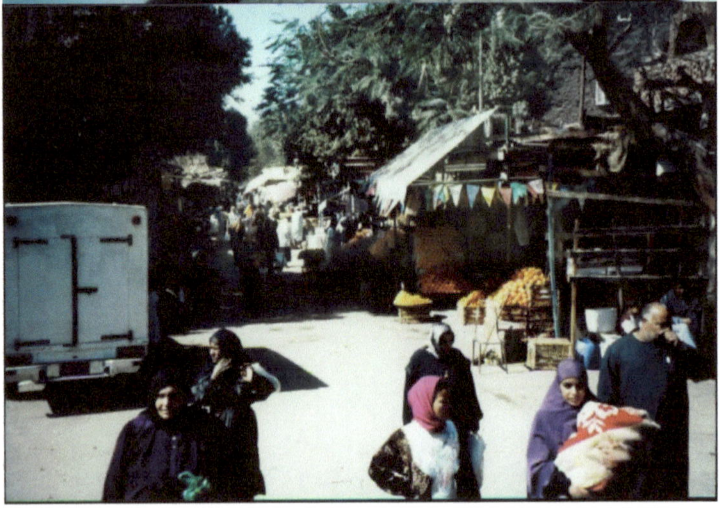

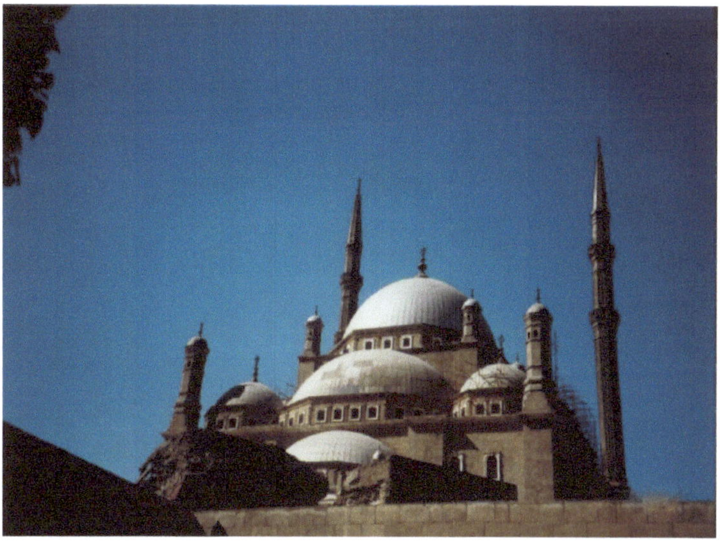

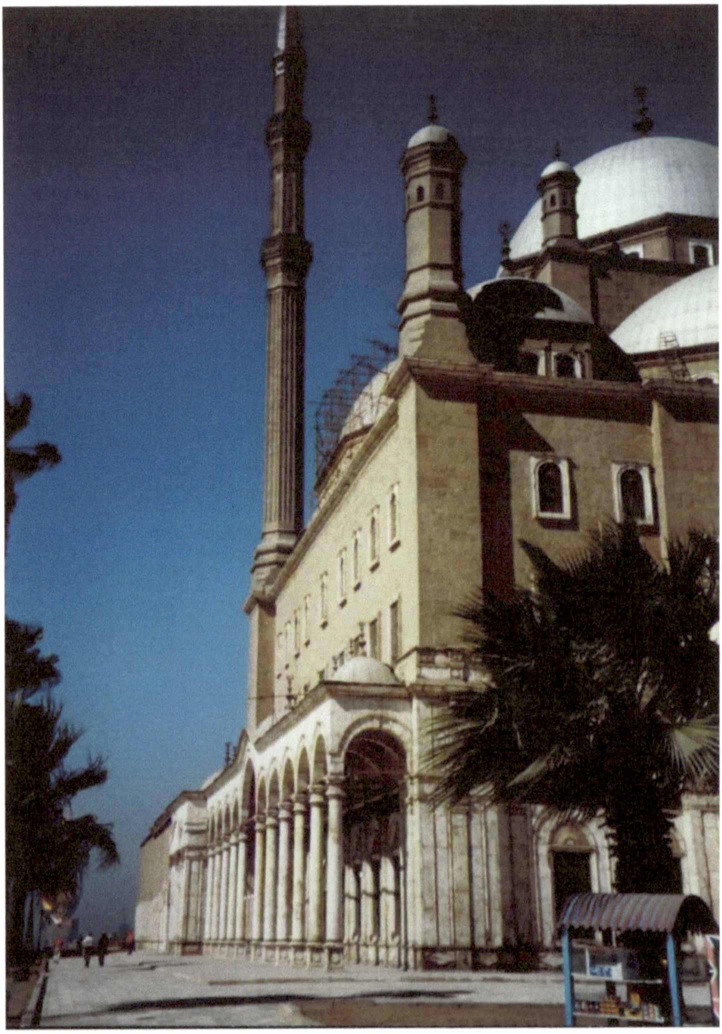

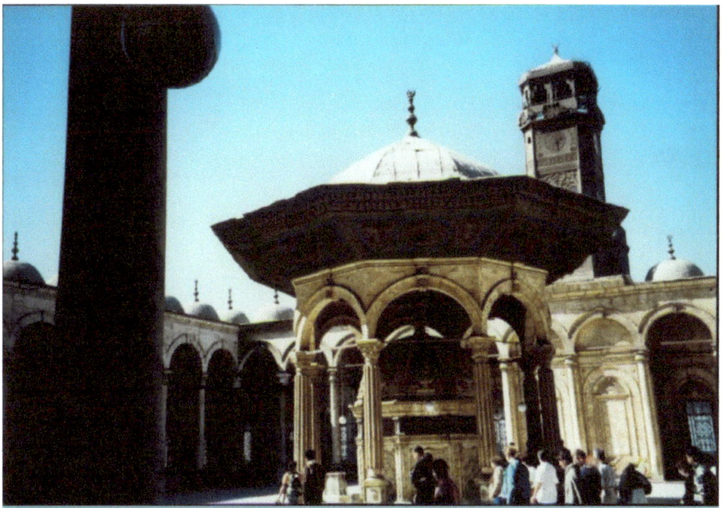

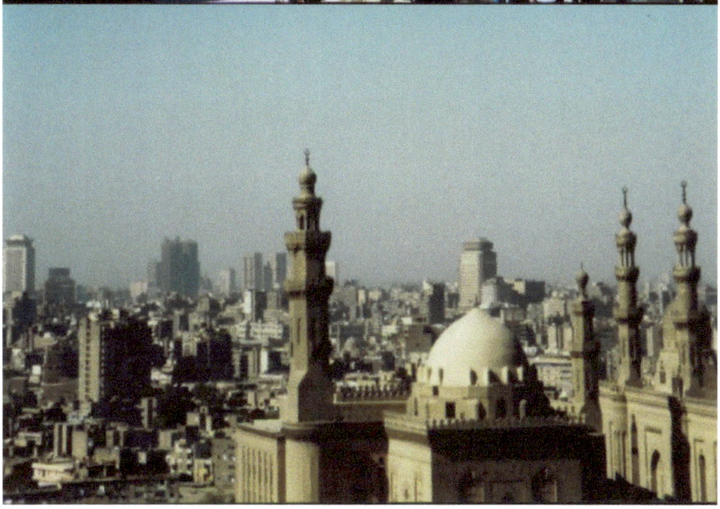

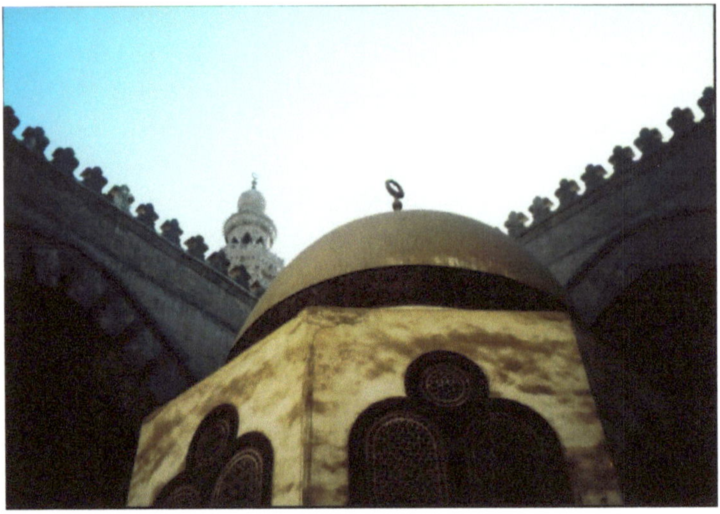

www.ingramcontent.com/pod-product-compliance
Lightning Source LLC
Chambersburg PA
CBHW040828180526
45159CB00001B/110
9781514300046